BLACK
NOVEMBER

BLACK NOVEMBER

THE CARL D. BRADLEY TRAGEDY

Andrew Kantar

Michigan State University Press • *East Lansing*

⊖ The paper used in this publication meets the minimum requirements
of ANSI/NISO Z39.48-1992 (R 1997) (Permanence of Paper).

 Michigan State University Press
East Lansing, Michigan 48823-5245
www.msupress.msu.edu

Printed and bound in the United States of America.

12 11 10 09 08 07 06   1 2 3 4 5 6 7 8 9 0

LIBRARY OF CONGRESS CATALOGING-IN-PUBLICATION DATA
Kantar, Andrew Klekner.
Black November : the Carl D. Bradley tragedy / Andrew Kantar.
p. cm.
Includes bibliographical references.
ISBN-13: 978-0-87013-783-9 (pbk. 13dig : alk. paper)
ISBN-10: 0-87013-783-2 (pbk. 10dig : alk. paper)
1. Carl D. Bradley (Ship) 2. Shipwrecks—Michigan, Lake. 3. Survival after
airplane accidents, shipwrecks, etc.—Michigan, Lake. I. Title.
G520.C2958K36 2006
917.7404—dc22
2006021614

Cover and book design by Sharp Des!gns, Inc., Lansing, Michigan

<Cover art credit>

green press Michigan State University Press is a member of the Green Press
INITIATIVE Initiative and is committed to developing and encouraging eco-
logically responsible publishing practices. For more information about the
Green Press Initiative and the use of recycled paper in book publishing, please
visit *www.greenpressinitiative.org*.

For Fran, my most trusted critic.

CONTENTS

ACKNOWLEDGMENTS

The generosity, knowledge, and expertise of several individuals helped me complete this book. First, I gratefully acknowledge and thank my editors at MSU Press, Julie Loehr and Martha Bates, for their editorial insights, their sense of humor, and perhaps most of all, for their literary vision and recognition of the value of nonfiction for young adults.

It is important and appropriate to recognize the extraordinary narrative of *Bradley* survivor Frank Mays, as documented in his book, *If We Make it 'til Daylight* (co-authored by Jim and Pat Stayer and Tim Juhl). His firsthand account proved valuable in reconstructing events surrounding the *Bradley* tragedy.

I offer warmest heartfelt thanks to the following family members of the *Bradley*'s crew: Charlie and Nancy Horn, Betty and Bob Kowalski, Michael Vogler, and Janet Enos.

Also, Mark Thompson, shipwreck author, historian and Rogers City native, deserves recognition and a special debt of gratitude for his candid and thoughtful commentary on the manuscript.

Thank you to Richard Lamb and Bill Valentine, both of the *Presque Isle Advance* newspaper, for their cooperation in sharing the historical archives of original newspaper issues and for generously reproducing photographs and permitting their reprint in this publication. The following librarians and archivists also provided valuable assistance: Laural Maldonado, Charla Kramer, Carrie Forbes, Pat Oldfield, Barbara Giles-Lemmon, David Poremba, and Mary Wallace.

I wish to express special thanks to Sally, Max, and Emily for their love and support. Finally, I thank my wife, Fran, for her unflagging patience, sound judgment, and faith.

BLACK
NOVEMBER

CHAPTER ONE

GREAT WATER

The Great Lakes of North America are some of Earth's most impressive treasures left to us by the massive glaciers of the Ice Age 11,000 years ago. Stretching 1,160 miles from New York to Minnesota, these magnificent fresh water seas have at once fascinated, terrified, and beckoned us for centuries. Composed of five bodies, they are, from east to west, Lake Ontario, Lake Erie, Lake Huron, Lake Michigan, and Lake Superior.

If you were to make a Great Lakes' journey, following the shoreline of all five lakes, you would pass the states of Minnesota, Wisconsin, Michigan, Illinois, Indiana, Ohio, Pennsylvania, and New York, and the Canadian province of Ontario. The entire voyage (including islands) would take you a staggering 9,700 miles! And the states you would visit account for one-third of our nation's population. In fact, some of North America's major metropolitan areas developed on the shores of the Great Lakes—Chicago, Milwaukee, Detroit, Cleveland, and Toronto.

Together, these lakes comprise twenty percent of the world's fresh water. In addition, many state and national parks along their shores attest to their recreational and historical value. Each year tourists trek to Lake Superior's mysterious Pictured Rocks or to the untamed wilderness of Isle Royale. Many are drawn to Lake Michigan's famous sand dunes, such as the mythical Sleeping Bear Dunes, and every year thousands are transported back in time on Lake Huron's historic Mackinac Island.

The lakes have also served as the water highways of commerce, making a vital connection between the Northeast and Midwest. The workhorses on these routes are huge freighters that haul iron ore, limestone, coal, grain, and petroleum. These giants of the lakes, sometimes longer than three football fields, sail the inland seas with crews of skilled and hard-working men.

Most of us look out from the shore of the endless body of water until it meets the horizon, marveling at its sheer size. We experience the lakes in summer, feeling the cool, refreshing one-foot waves lapping gently as the sun reflects its warmth off of the water. But the captain and crew of the steamship freighters are aware of another side of these awesome waters, and it is something for which they have a great deal of respect. They have seen how quickly the lake's personality can change. Working a season that goes well into the treacherous month of November, those who sail the lakes have experienced the pitching and rolling of their ship in the teeth of strong winds and massive waves. They know the dangers that may lie ahead and of the thousands of vessels that never made port.

Lake Michigan, whose name comes from the Algonquian word *michigami,* meaning "Great Water," is the only Great Lake that resides entirely within American boundaries, providing scenic coastline for Michigan, Indiana, Illinois, and Wisconsin. Only Lake Superior is deeper, and in terms of size, Lake Michigan is just slightly smaller than Lake Huron. Lake Michigan is as much as 923 feet deep, and its spectacular shoreline extends more than 1,600 miles (including islands).

Imagine luxuriating on soft, sandy beaches, photographing spectacular sunsets from the Michigan shore, fishing for trophy salmon, exploring islands large and small, or visiting a coastal resort that offers sailing, swimming, hiking, biking—just about any outdoor activity. Because of its extraordinary natural beauty, Lake Michigan has become a recreational paradise.

Lake Michigan, however, is not "all play and no work." It is also a busy shipping route. American and international freighters that travel these pathways of commerce have contributed to the growth and prosperity of cities such as Chicago and Milwaukee. Each of these freighters is capable of delivering thousands of tons of cargo to a destination. Their cargo of iron ore and limestone led to the production of steel for burgeoning industry along the lake. The Great Water has indeed served us well for many generations.

But all of this has not come without a price. Lake Michigan is known for violent and destructive storms that can develop without warning and with devastating consequences. For this reason, seamen have long held a special respect for the Great Water. According to shipwreck expert William Ratigan, Lake Michigan's unique storm patterns may be attributed to its long shape, which allows winds to push the length of the lake, raising the big water higher and higher. And when the storms begin to howl, Lake Michigan offers very few natural harbors for safety, making it doubly hazardous.

One of the first ships to sail the Great Water was the *Griffon,* which was built by the wealthy French explorer René-Robert Cavalier de La Salle, and sailed Lake Michigan in 1679. Named after the mythical creature that was half eagle and half lion, the *Griffon* was a small, handsome craft, only about sixty feet from bow to stern. After some rough going on Lake Erie, the *Griffon* made a difficult voyage across Lake Huron, all the way to Green Bay on Lake Michigan. She began her return trip without La Salle and loaded with a heavy cargo of beaver pelts. Steering a course around the islands of upper Lake Michigan, through the Straits of Mackinac to Lake Huron, she encountered a fierce September storm that lasted four days. She was never heard from again.

The *Griffon* disappeared without a trace, becoming the first shipwreck on the Great Lakes. Sadly, it would be the first of over 10,000 wrecks, the bones of broken ships, scattered across the muddy bottoms in silent testimony to the centuries of devastation brought on by the lakes' violent moods.

Knowing its unpredictable nature and sudden storms, it comes as no surprise that Lake Michigan has a long history of shipwrecks and maritime tragedy. Many of these vessels simply disappeared after being dragged down to Michigan's great depths, never to be found. Few would remember the schooner *Black Hawk* that sank in November of 1847, or the steamer *Omar Pasha* that was lost eight years later in the same deadly month. Another schooner, *Thomas Hume,* disappeared in May of 1891, and in late October of 1898, the *L.R. Doty,* a steamer, was forever lost with all hands. The Great Storm of 1913 marked one of the most brutal weeks in shipwreck history. Throughout the November siege, the Great Lakes, particularly Lake Huron, were relentlessly battered, taking the horrific toll of hundreds of lives and millions of dollars in lost or damaged ships and cargo.

One of Lake Michigan's most famous storms was the Armistice Day Storm of 1940. On the eleventh of November, that most treacherous of all months, there were reports of wind gusts ranging from 70 to 125 miles per hour and waves more than thirty-five feet high. That day, three ships were lost to the sea. Two steamers, the *Anna C. Minch* and *William B. Davock,* were sailing the same waters on the eastern side of Lake Michigan when tragedy struck. Both disappeared without a trace. There is some speculation that the two may have collided, causing the *Minch* to lose her stern. Others believe that the two were actually four hours apart and disappeared for different reasons. The *Minch,* they speculate, developed a huge crack in her hull due to the heavy pounding of the seas. This could have led to a structural failure that would have caused the ship to break in two. Those same violent waters might have battered some of the *Davock*'s hatch covers open, allowing massive amounts of water to enter. One thing is certain. No one lived to tell the story. On that day, the entire crew of both ships, including twenty-four men on the *Minch* and the *Davock*'s crew of thirty-two, vanished.

During that same terrible storm, the crew of the *Novadoc* would face its own struggle for survival. Sailing north, along the eastern shore of Lake Michigan, the 250-foot vessel encountered the very storm that swallowed the giant steamers *Minch* and *Davock*. The *Novadoc*'s captain attempted to turn the ship around, but the high water would not allow it. The embattled ship was in view of the red-brick Little Sable Point Lighthouse as the sea relentlessly pushed it toward the shore. The seas were so rough that when the *Novadoc* would dip into a wave's trough, the lighthouse would actually vanish from sight, only to reappear when the ship reached the crest. Eyewitness accounts describe waves "like mountains" that were so powerful they exploded the windows in the ship's wheelhouse, causing it to flood. The keeper of the lighthouse sent word to the Coast Guard station at Ludington as the captain and crew of the *Novadoc* fought for their lives. Eventually, the crippled vessel ran aground on an offshore sandbar and broke in half. But the crew's ordeal was just beginning.

For thirty-six hours the cold and hungry crew huddled together, first in the captain's cabin, only to later be forced into the captain's office when the cabin door caved in. This was their last remaining refuge, and together, they resorted to breaking and burning sticks of furniture to stay warm, in the hope that somehow they would be rescued. A crowd of hundreds gathered on shore, watching helplessly as the human drama played out before their eyes. Two nights passed without rescue. The men, who had nothing to eat for two days, kept sending up rockets to signal to those onshore that they were still alive. Before help arrived, the men mourned the loss of two of their crew who were swept overboard by a giant wave.

Tired of watching and waiting, three brave fishermen decided to take action. Piloting their boat, *Three Brothers,* through the still-raging waters, they risked their lives to rescue the imperiled men. The *Novadoc*'s captain and crew remained forever grateful to the three courageous fishermen who saved their lives during the Armistice Day Storm of 1940.

It is a well-known fact that in November the Great Lakes spawn storms of unimaginable fury. A legendary struggle unfolds when these great seas unleash their wrath upon the giant freighters that bravely endure gale-force winds and tall water. It is a struggle of epic proportions, man against nature, life and death. There are no higher stakes than survival.

The three most dramatic and horrifying ordeals on the Great Lakes have taken place on Lake Superior, Lake Huron, and Lake Michigan. Many people are familiar with the tragic loss of the steamer *Edmund Fitzgerald,* which disappeared on November 10, 1975, during a monster storm on Lake Superior. This is the most famous shipwreck in Great Lakes history. The end came so quickly for the 729-foot giant, she never even sent out a distress call. Just seventeen miles from the safety of Whitefish Point, suddenly and without warning, the *Fitzgerald* dropped from sight off of the radar screen of the *Arthur Anderson,* the freighter that was following her. All twenty-nine men aboard perished.

Some believe that the *Fitzgerald,* after coming too close to a shallow point near Caribou Island, called Six-Fathom Shoal, might have scraped bottom, causing damage to her hull. Others theorize that the combined effects of taking in water through her hatches and the huge waves washing across her deck pulled her bow beneath the surface, propelling the *Fitzgerald* 500 feet to Lake Superior's muddy bottom. Upon impact, it is argued, the *Fitzgerald* then broke apart, perhaps exploding, leaving the bow upright and the stern inverted. But despite subsequent visits to the wreck site, to this day the cause of her sinking remains a mystery.

Before the loss of the *Fitzgerald,* the 601-foot *Daniel J. Morrell* was lost on Lake Huron, close to Michigan's "thumb." In her more than sixty years of service, the *Morrell* had survived storms with winds of 100 miles per hour. But Lake Huron's storm of November 28–29, 1966, was to be different. The *Morrell* had been sailing about twenty miles ahead of the *Edward Y. Townsend* when her failure to answer her sister ship raised concerns. On November 30 the *Morrell* had failed to radio in a required morning report. By then, nobody had a clue as to the whereabouts of the *Morrell.*

A Coast Guard search on November 30 located a raft that held four men from the *Morrell.* Three were dead, but one miraculously survived the ordeal. Dennis Hale, a 26-year-old deckhand and the father of four children, suffered from frostbite and hypothermia, but was the sole survivor of a storm that claimed the lives of the other twenty-eight members of *Morrell*'s crew. It was later concluded that this majestic freighter had snapped in two during the November terror of 1966 due to her brittle, steel hull. Remarkably, after the bow sank, the stern continued past it, propelling the back half of the ship five miles before it, too, sank.

Before Lake Superior's wreck of the *Fitzgerald* and Lake Huron's destruction of the *Morrell* came Lake Michigan's assault on the *Carl D. Bradley,* the record-setting limestone carrier from Rogers City, Michigan. It is the largest ship to sink in Lake Michigan and one of the most famous shipwrecks in Great Lakes history. One cold and stormy November night in 1958, the captain and crew of the S.S. *Carl D. Bradley* struggled in terror against a violent, storm-tossed Lake Michigan. By the time the lake calmed, the *Bradley,* a fallen giant, rested in two pieces, 365 feet below. A grieving town would mourn the loss of thirty-three men and listen in horror to the tale of the two survivors. On that black November night, a lake, a ship, and a town would be unhappily intertwined, forever woven into the fabric of Great Lakes lore.

CHAPTER TWO

THE NAUTICAL CITY

"**W**elcome to Rogers City—the Nautical City." That is the message on the sign that greets you as you enter the city limits of Rogers City, Michigan. Located on the shores of Lake Huron, at the northern reaches of Michigan's Lower Peninsula, this place could be called the little town on the big lake. With one stoplight, one movie theater, and a population of about 4,000, this sleepy little community is the epitome of small-town America. Well-maintained brick and clapboard homes with neatly trimmed lawns line the residential streets that ultimately lead you down to the shores of the Great Lake.

On a cool summer's evening you might take a walk down to Lakeside Park, along the marina, where dozens of sailboats and fishing boats are lined up awaiting tomorrow's activities. Families wander the park, eating ice cream and hot dogs. A band might be performing a concert in the open band shell, or parents and grandparents could be watching their favorite Little League teams playing on one of four diamonds, so close to Lake Huron that the outfielders hear the waves slapping the shoreline. It is the sort of place where everyone knows everyone else—their family, their church, their graduating class, and who they married.

Rogers City is also home to the world's largest limestone quarry, which is located just a couple of miles down the road, at the Port of

Calcite. It is there that a harbor was created for the giant stone-carrying freighters to take on their cargo for departure to the steel mills along the lakes. All of this made Rogers City not only a world center for limestone processing but also home port to a fleet of freighters.

Growing up in this port city, boys saw their dads, uncles, cousins, and brothers go to sea. They would be away for long stretches of time, and for the residents of Rogers City, working on the big freighters was a way of life for generations. Each family's sacrifice was significant. Fathers would often miss their children's school activities, even holiday celebrations and birthdays. Indeed, sometimes the men were out to sea during the birth of their children! But that was day-to-day life for the families of this seafaring town, and it was accepted. It was not unusual for boys, when they turned sixteen, to drop out of high school and join the fleet. After all, the pay was considered good, and it was a life they had grown up knowing. So began many careers aboard the freighters, careers that would sometimes span more than 35 years.

The women of Rogers City were sometimes referred to as the un-sung heroes of this unorthodox lifestyle. They were strong, independent individuals, who often married at a young age, and as children they were just as familiar as their brothers with the unusual demands this existence placed on family, especially their mothers. Because the men were absent so much of the time, their wives and mothers had to be unusually self-reliant. They managed their households, raising the children, paying the bills and keeping the budget, taking the children to the doctor, and attending to all school matters. At times, the responsibility must have seemed overwhelming, for many of these women raised six, seven, even eight children! But these mothers did have at least one "ace in the hole": when their children misbehaved, they could fall back on the threat, "Wait until your father gets home!" At night, when the children were tucked safely in their beds, their mothers would say a prayer before going to sleep, a prayer that God would protect the sailors, keep them safe, and bring them home. Life in this town was not easy by any means, but there was a true sense of family and community.

Founded on July 13, 1871, Rogers City was named for William E. Rogers of New York, the man who then owned the land. The land was dense with pine forests, and it was so swampy and spongy that ditches had to be dug to drain off water before it could be settled. The region had previously been inhabited by the Chippewa Indians, who mostly used the land for hunting.

The Chippewa had considered the place sacred. Once a year, all the Chippewa men, women, and children made a long journey to the mouth of the Ocqueoc River, and then slowly walked, following the long, winding course, to where the river's mouth spills into Lake Huron. Once there, they celebrated, with much dancing and eating. At the celebration's dramatic climax, the old, the sick, and the crippled left their families and entered the river's swift currents, allowing their weak bodies to be carried into the Great Lake. For hundreds of years, crippled children and sickly grandparents were subjected to this brutal custom, and although it seems to us to be an act of inconceivable heartlessness, it was done willingly. To them, it was an expression of selfless devotion to family, intended to spare their loved ones the responsibility of caring for them. It must have been perceived as a dignified departure, one that the tribe should not mourn, but rather rejoice.

For decades, lumbering and fishing were the primary industries of the region, but at the turn of the twentieth century it became clear that Rogers City was sitting on top of remarkably vast stores of limestone. In 1907 H. H. Hindshaw, a geologist from New York, sensed the great value of this resource and purchased 600 acres of limestone-rich land next to the city. In 1910 some New York financiers formed Michigan Limestone and Chemical Company of Calcite, and purchased an additional 8,000 acres as well as a stone crusher capable of crushing up to ten million pounds of limestone in a day. The next year, a man from Chicago arrived, a man whose name would become legend in the town of Rogers City. His name was Carl David Bradley.

As the new manager of Michigan Limestone and Chemical Company, Carl Bradley wasted little time in getting the plant up and running.

A great innovator and tireless organizer, Bradley started out by bringing in 1,200 Polish, German, and Italian immigrant workers to build the business that had, up to this point, little more than a name. A quarry was already operating, but Bradley's job was to turn it into something much grander. The immigrant workers built the offices, the railroads, and the power plant needed to support the quarry's expansion. The power plant generated enough energy to service not only the limestone operation but also the entire town of Rogers City.

Of course, the company needed a way to transport thousands of tons of stone to mills for processing into steel. Bradley's answer for that was to build a harbor at the quarry for loading huge freighters that would haul the stone. But who would run the shipping of this heavy cargo? Bradley believed that he could do that, too. In 1912, when the limestone operation was in full swing, Bradley founded and became president of the Bradley Transportation Company and began building a fleet of freighters. He was now running both Michigan Limestone and Bradley Transportation.

Bradley's freighters were truly distinctive in that they were self-unloading ships, which means pretty much what it sounds like. They were capable of unloading their own cargo. Unlike the "straight deckers" that were then common on the lakes, Bradley's boats were equipped with a long "boom" or conveyor-belt arm that could be used to move the cargo off the ship.

Self-unloading systems use a series of conveyors to move cargo from below deck to the dock. The process begins well below the deck, in the vast, dark hull of the ship. The hull is divided into compartments, and each compartment has ten hatches. These hatches slope down, allowing the cargo of stone or coal to slide down into a square-shaped pocket. From there, air-operated gates send the cargo to two tunnel belts that run lengthwise along each side of the ship (port and starboard). These below-deck tunnel belts carry the stone to the forward end of the ship, up an incline, eventually dumping it into two V-shaped chutes. The stone is then deposited into giant, eight-foot-wide buckets, called elevator buckets. These massive buckets revolve on a chain, much like the seats of a Ferris wheel. The elevator buckets carry the stone up to the deck, dropping their contents onto the final stage: the boom belt. This is the on-deck conveyor that is located on the boom or long arm that is visible on the decks of these great vessels. Once the cargo reaches the boom belt, the long arm can be swung to port (left) or starboard (right), to deposit the cargo dockside.

Straight deckers were limited to unloading only at docks that had the equipment needed to remove the ship's cargo. Using this equipment was a long process, taking up to twelve or thirteen hours. By contrast, the self-unloading freighters could perform the task in about four hours, nearly one-third of the time. In addition, self-unloaders were more versatile, capable of depositing crushed stone on a dock, at a warehouse, or in railcars. Bradley knew that the time-saving capabilities of the self-unloading freighters would enable them to make more runs and deliveries to ports that did not have unloading equipment. History proved him right; almost all of the old straight deckers have vanished from the industry, having been either equipped with self-unloading systems or replaced entirely.

Known as a gregarious, charming man, Bradley also was said to have been kind and generous. People still recall the way that he could handle problems with compassion and creativity. When the immigrants were brought in to work on the construction of the plant, the sudden increase in population caused a milk shortage. The workers' children were not able to get the milk that was so important to their health and well being. Again, Bradley had the solution. He started a dairy farm and called it Bradley Farms, and that was the end of the milk crisis.

Bradley's plan for Rogers City was indeed a bold one. It quickly became home to the world's largest limestone mining operation, producing and shipping more than 700 million tons of limestone since its inception. Before it became the "Nautical City," Rogers City was known as the "Limestone City." The limestone and shipping industries breathed life into the little town's economy, translating into jobs for the townspeople. In fact, one in five citizens was employed by either Michigan Limestone or Bradley Transportation.

In 1928 the community was shocked by the sudden and unexpected death of Carl Bradley. At sixty-eight years of age, he suffered a stroke and was gone. But his memory lived on long after he died, and to this day, the citizens of Rogers City speak fondly of the man who brought industry and prosperity to their hometown.

CHAPTER THREE

A GIANT IS BORN

In 1927 the New York Yankees ruled as baseball's World Series Champions. Known as the "greatest team of all time," they were led by the legendary powerhouse, Babe Ruth, who hit a record-setting sixty home runs. That same year, another record-setting powerhouse was born: The *Carl D. Bradley*. And she was a giant in every sense of the word.

At 639 feet long, longer than two football fields, the *Bradley* wielded 5,000 horsepower. Fully loaded, she could move along at fourteen miles per hour, a pretty good clip for a freighter. Launched on April 9, 1927, in Lorain, Ohio, she became the longest, most powerful vessel to sail the Great Lakes. If you could have stood her on end, she would have reached skyscraper heights of sixty-four stories! That's taller than the famous St. Louis Arch at its highest point. But the *Bradley* was not just big and powerful, she was also widely viewed as being the safest ship on the lakes. In fact, many thought her to be unsinkable.

Built by the American Ship Building yard, the *Bradley,* like her namesake, was destined for great things. Right from the start everyone knew she was something special. On her very first run, at the end of July, she made a record-setting haul, and then simply went on to break her own records. On May 9, 1929, she stunned the industry, delivering a mammoth cargo of 18,114 tons of limestone to Gary, Indiana. That was enough limestone to fill more than 300 railcars! No other freighter would be able to duplicate this feat for the next thirteen years.

The *Bradley* was one of nine ships in the Bradley Transportation fleet. All of Bradley's boats were "self-unloaders." The *Bradley* would load at the Port of Calcite, her home port in Rogers City. From there she would make deliveries to ports on Lake Michigan and Lake Erie. The limestone she carried was used in the agricultural and pharmaceutical industries, as well as for making steel and cement for construction.

By 1954 Captain Roland Bryan was master of the *Bradley*. Bryan, a native of Ontario, Canada, made his home in Loudonville, New York. A 38-year veteran of the lakes, he became a sailor in 1920, at the age of fourteen. For seventeen years he served as a first mate in the Bradley Transportation fleet, and he served as captain for another seven. The *Bradley*'s chief engineer was Raymond Buehler, from Lakeville, Ohio, a seasoned veteran, who served on the *Bradley* almost from the day she was launched. By the time he became chief engineer, Buehler probably knew her as well or better than anyone.

Including the captain, the *Bradley* operated with a crew of thirty-five men, 90 percent of whom were from Michigan. Twenty-five of them came from Rogers City, so three out of four men on the *Bradley* called that little town of 3,873 their home. It is no wonder they were such a tightly knit group. They attended school together, married classmates, and generally grew up together.

They were single and married; their children were as young as a one-month-old baby and on up. Each seaman had family and friends who anxiously anticipated the end of the 1958 shipping season and prayed for his safe return. Each one had a story, a reason for being there. The youngest member of the crew was James Selke, an 18-year-old teenager who was working to save up money for college. At sixty-three years old, John Zoho, the ship's steward (cook), was the oldest member on board. Wheelsman Joseph Krawczak was looking forward to being reunited with his wife and six children. His family knew that the seasonal life of a steamboat man would regularly take him away from home, but always with the expectation that he would come back. Together, the *Bradley*'s crew and their families would happily anticipate the season's final voyage that would deliver to them a wonderfully long winter lay-up.

Two men who might have normally been aboard for that final run were George Sobeck Jr. and his uncle, Sylvester "Wes" Sobeck. But in a strange twist of fate, they stayed behind for the funeral of George's dad and Wes' brother—a funeral that might have saved their lives.

So, with a measure of confidence and a healthy dose of faith, the crew of the *Bradley* prepared to make one last November run, departing Rogers City, traveling down Lake Michigan to Buffington, Indiana, the delivery port for the industrial city of Gary. But before the 1958 season's finale, some concerns regarding the *Bradley*'s condition began to surface.

Despite her great success and record-setting runs, it was not always smooth sailing for the *Bradley*. Many times she endured and survived the Great Lakes' brutal assaults. And Captain Bryan nursed her through various mishaps and incidents in the years immediately preceding her last voyage in November of 1958.

To be sure, the *Bradley* had suffered her share of bumps and bruises, nothing very unusual for a ship of her size and age, but enough to require some patching. For example, in April of 1956, while sailing down the St. Clair River near Detroit, she collided with *White Rose,* a Canadian vessel. She sustained relatively minor damage near her middle, in the vicinity of cargo hatch number ten on her starboard (right) side. A year after the incident, some hairline cracks on the hull, up to six feet long, suggested that the collision damage may have been more extensive than originally believed. These cracks were repaired.

Twice in 1958 the *Bradley* actually touched bottom at Cedarville, Michigan. The first time was in May and caused minor damage. The second grounding, just a couple of weeks before her final November journey, ruptured her steel bottom plates, requiring an eighteen-hour welding job to repair the damage. Neither of these groundings was thought significant enough to be reported to the Coast Guard.

At thirty-one years of age, the *Bradley* was certainly not considered old, but she did show some wear. Most notably, the hull showed signs of leaking and the cargo hold was in rough shape and needed to be replaced. Her owners had agreed to have a new cargo hold installed in the off-season, at a cost of around $800,000. In addition, her bulkheads were said to have rusted so badly that you could actually see from one compartment into another. In fact, deck watch Frank Mays said that the *Bradley*'s crew used to joke that "the old girl was held together by rust."

And that was not all. The *Bradley*'s ballast tanks were leaking, requiring the pumps to run almost constantly. The ballast tanks are designed to hold thousands of tons of water which are used to stabilize an empty ship. It was also noted that she had popped a lot of rivets, which had been replaced with bolts. The ship's steel plates were securely riveted, but in the course of thousands of miles, the pressure of the pounding seas can essentially fire these rivets right off. It has been said that so many rivets pop off of a ship's steel plates during a rough journey that you could actually gather buckets full of them. Ideally, it would be better to replace the rivets with more of the same but sometimes bolts can adequately hold a hull's steel plates in place. Individually, these issues proved of little concern, but cumulatively, one has to wonder just how much stress the *Bradley* could take.

Mid-November, 1958, after a season of forty-five successful round-trips and more than 27,000 miles, Captain Bryan was prepared to take the *Bradley* out on one final voyage for the season. Privately, in a November 8 letter to Florence Herd, his girlfriend from Port Huron, Michigan, Captain Bryan acknowledged his concerns about the *Bradley:* "This boat is getting pretty ripe for too much weather. I'll be glad when they get her fixed up." In another letter, to Ken Faweet, his best friend, Captain Bryan confided that the *Bradley*'s "hull is not good . . . badly damaged at Cedarville."

Nevertheless, at the time of her final sailing, the *Bradley* was deemed seaworthy, passing the U.S. Coast Guard's safety inspections, as well as being certified by Lloyd's Register of Shipping and Inspection. Incredibly, between 1955 and 1957, the Bradley Transportation Line's nine-ship fleet had logged in more than two-million man hours without injury! This re-markable record earned them the National Safety Council's award of honor. In fact, Bradley Transportation had never lost a ship since its incep-tion in 1912. In 1958, the *Carl D. Bradley* was part of the world's safest fleet of freighters.

CHAPTER FOUR

HEADING HOME

The day was Monday, November 17, 1958, and the *Bradley* was making her forty-sixth and final voyage of the shipping season. The trip down Michigan's west coast to the U.S. Steel mill in Gary, Indiana, was without incident. She had just finished unloading her cargo, and the limestone rolled off the boom's conveyor in a fairly quick six hours. It was now time to think about heading home.

At this very moment, much of the rest of the country was in the throes of a terrible storm. In true November fashion, a warm-air mass from the south had collided with cold air from the north, wreaking havoc across a swath that cut from the Canadian border down to Mexico. Tucson, Arizona, received six inches of snow, and parts of Nevada reported sub-zero temperatures. Twenty inches of snow were dumped on southern Wyoming, and the Dakotas were trying to dig their way out of sixteen inches, as strong winds slashed across the plains. The storm left people stranded, missing, or dead in several states. But blizzard conditions were not the only concern. As it moved eastward, the massive system also spawned thirty-five tornadoes, devastating Texas, Oklahoma, Missouri, Kansas, Minnesota, Iowa, and Illinois. Whether the crew of the *Bradley* knew it or not, one of the fiercest monster storms of the century was headed their way.

At 8:00 P.M. Captain Bryan heard the weather forecast and it was not good. Winds of fifty to sixty-five miles per hour from the south were predicted, and this would whip up waves of considerable height on Lake Michigan. But Captain Bryan knew that the *Bradley* had weathered storms before, even this season, and had always come through safely. Besides, the crew would be anxious to return to their loved ones, and the final destination of Rogers City would take most of them practically to their doorsteps. If all went well, they could make it home in about thirty hours.

Before departure, as the ship was completing its unloading, Captain Bryan discussed the planned course for the return trip with First Mate Elmer Fleming. Because the winds were from the south and would be shifting southwest, it made sense to take the *Bradley* along Wisconsin's coast, using its shoreline as protection. When they reached Cana Island, located in the northern end of the lake, they would make their move toward the Michigan side of the lake. Cutting a northeast path toward Lansing Shoal, past the chain of islands called "the Beavers," they would use the southwest winds as a tail-wind advantage. They would have to exercise caution near the Beaver chain of islands, carefully avoiding the treacherous Boulder Reef that was nearby. From there they would then make their way toward the Straits of Mackinac, right on through to Lake Huron, and home to Rogers City. At least that was the plan. The most hazardous stretch would be negotiating in high seas the ninety miles separating the shores of Wisconsin and Michigan.

At about 10:00 P.M., the evening of November 17, the winds were only twenty-five to thirty-five miles per hour and the lake was calm. The *Carl D. Bradley* left the port of Buffington, just outside of Gary, Indiana, and began her final journey, carrying 9,000 tons of water in the ballast tanks for added stability. Following the Wisconsin shoreline all night, the ship passed Milwaukee at about 4:00 A.M. It was now Tuesday, November 18, and the *Bradley* was eleven miles from shore and moving along at a steady fifteen miles per hour. By 7:00 A.M., she was about seven miles off the shore of Sheboygan, along with two other freighters who were going the same way but hugging the shoreline more closely. That morning, gale warnings were posted, and it was not long before conditions deteriorated.

The S.S. *Carl D. Bradley* in her prime. Courtesy of the Presque Isle County Historical Museum.

The *Carl D. Bradley* of Rogers City. Courtesy of Jack Deo, Superior View Historic Photography and Art Gallery.

"Mayday! Mayday!" First Mate Elmer Fleming's urgent call for help was received over this Coast Guard radio. Courtesy of the *Presque Isle County Advance.*

The 180-foot Coast Guard cutter *Sundew.* Courtesy of the *Presque Isle County Advance.*

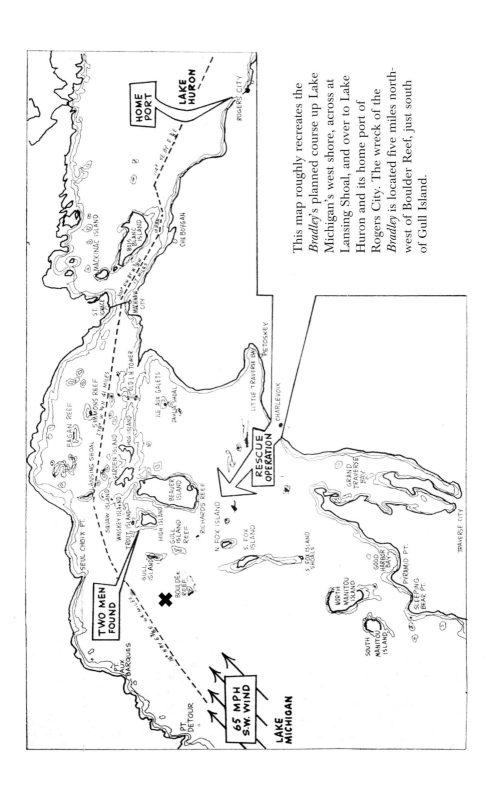

This map roughly recreates the *Bradley*'s planned course up Lake Michigan's west shore, across at Lansing Shoal, and over to Lake Huron and its home port of Rogers City. The wreck of the *Bradley* is located five miles northwest of Boulder Reef, just south of Gull Island.

The *Carl D. Bradley* on the Detroit River. The Ambassador Bridge, which connects Detroit, Michigan and Windsor, Ontario, is in the background. Courtesy of the Burton Historical Collection, Detroit Public Library.

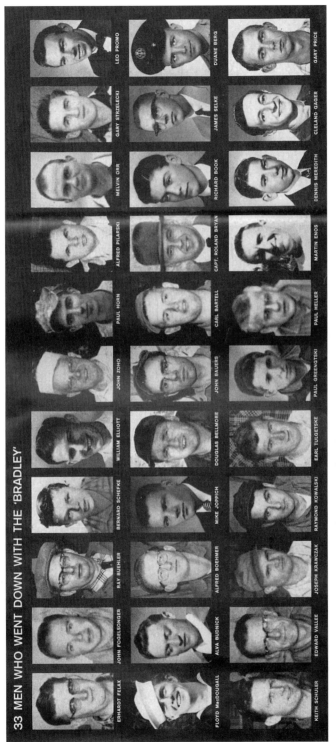

33 MEN WHO WENT DOWN WITH THE 'BRADLEY'

ERHARDT FELAX — JOHN FOGELSONGER — RAY BUEHLER — BERNARD SCHEFKE — WILLIAM ELLIOTT — JOHN ZOHO — PAUL HORN — ALFRED PILARSKI — MELVIN ORR — GARY STRZELECKI — LEO PROMO

FLOYD MacDOUGALL — ALVA BUDNICK — ALFRED BOEHMER — MIKE JOPPICH — DOUGLAS BELLMORE — JOHN BAUERS — CARL BARTELL — CAPT. ROLAND BRYAN — RICHARD BOOK — JAMES SELKE — DUANE BERG

KEITH SCHULER — EDWARD VALLEE — JOSEPH KRAWCZAK — RAYMOND KOWALSKI — EARL TULGETSKE — PAUL GRENGTSKI — PAUL HELLER — MARTIN ENOS — DENNIS MEREDITH — CLELAND GAGER — GARY PRICE

The faces of tragedy: The *Carl D. Bradley*'s thirty-three lost crewmen.

A Coast Guard 40-footer joins the rescue effort. Courtesy of the *Presque Isle County Advance.*

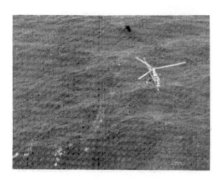

Searching for survivors. Photograph by *Bay City Times* reporter Gregg Smith and reprinted in the *Presque Isle County Advance.*

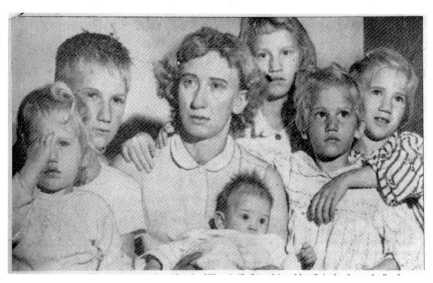

The wife and six children of 35-year-old wheelsman, Joe Krawczak. Lives were forever changed on that terrible November night. Courtesy of the *Presque Isle County Advance.*

Limp and exhausted from his fifteen-hour ordeal, survivor Frank Mays is carried aboard the *Sundew*. Courtesy of the *Presque Isle County Advance*.

Survivor Elmer Fleming is transported to a waiting ambulance. The 8' × 10' raft that saved both men is in the foreground.

A crowd in Charlevoix anxiously awaits the results of the Coast Guard's search-and-rescue mission. Courtesy of the *Presque Isle County Advance*.

Bodies recovered off Gull Island are placed aboard the *Sundew*.

Eighteen bodies of the *Bradley*'s crew were eventually recovered. Courtesy of the *Presque Isle County Advance*.

"A funeral on every street": Inside St. Ignatius Church in Rogers City, coffins fill the aisle as families and friends mourn the loss of nine crewmen.

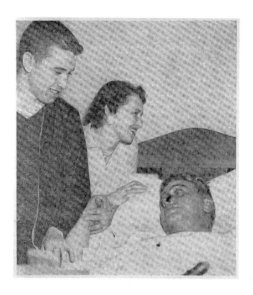

First Mate Elmer Fleming is shown here from his hospital bed with his wife Mary and son Douglas (15). Courtesy of the *Presque Isle County Advance.*

Still in their hospital robes, the *Bradley*'s only two survivors, Elmer Fleming (left) and Frank Mays are shown with members of the Coast Guard Marine Board of Investigation. Courtesy of Michael Vogler, Rogers City.

Just four months after the *Bradley* went down, Frank Mays looks over newspaper accounts of the event with his wife, Marlys, and sons (left to right) Michael (4), Frank Jr. (5 months), and Mark (2). Courtesy of Michael Vogler, Rogers City.

On August 9, 1987, the people of Rogers City unveiled this memorial to the men who perished on the *Bradley* and the *Cedarville*. Author's collection.

At about 1:15 P.M., the S.S. *Johnstown* was a few hours ahead of the *Bradley,* passing Boulder Reef near Gull Island (part of the Beaver chain of islands). They reported battling extraordinarily heavy seas of twenty-five-foot waves with wind gusts of seventy-five miles per hour. The *Bradley* was planning an identical route across the northern part of Lake Michigan. And in four short hours, the *Bradley*'s crew would be in that very spot, struggling for their lives against the raging sea.

By late afternoon, the *Bradley* and her crew found themselves in the middle of a full-blown storm with gale-force winds of sixty to sixty-five miles per hour and massive waves reaching a staggering twenty to twenty-five feet high! They were coming up on Cana Island, where, according to plan, the *Bradley* was going to make her northeasterly run past the Beaver Island chain and toward the Michigan side of the lake. It was a little before 4:00 P.M. when Captain Bryan, asked the ship's cook, John Zoho, to prepare an early dinner for the men. Knowing that this crossing was going to be rougher and more treacherous than it had been up the Wisconsin coast, Captain Bryan believed that an early dinner would allow Zoho time to secure everything in the ship's galley.

Zoho prepared a full meal consisting of hamburgers, fries, slices of cold tomato, sponge cake, and peaches. Up to this point, the *Bradley* was handling the rough water beautifully. Since she had no cargo, the *Bradley* was riding a little higher in the water and was, therefore, taking more of a pounding, but she was still riding smoothly. In fact, they did not even have to mount the sideboards on the mess hall tables to keep the plates from sliding around.

It was at about this time that a 26-year-old deck watchman named Frank Mays thought he had better get something in his stomach before he started his 4:00 P.M. to 8:00 P.M. watch shift. Seated at the mess table with his cousin, Alva Budnick, also twenty-six years old, the two enjoyed a somewhat hurried meal together. Zoho knew that the captain wanted the galley clean and secure before turning the ship toward the Michigan shore, so he urged the men to finish their dinners as quickly as possible.

Though the merciless pounding of the waves, not surprisingly, caused rivets to shoot off of the steel plates of the ship's hull, the *Bradley* was showing no signs of serious problems at this point. She was holding her own, and was actually proving to be flexible, just as she was designed to be. The large freighters of the lakes have been likened to great, towering skyscrapers, which are designed to bend, ever so slightly, in the wind. Following this principle, freighters' steel bodies also "flex" or "give" a little to reduce the sudden stress brought on by the tempestuous waters of a storm. Remarkably, this flexing has actually been observed by those on deck as a heaving or twisting motion, and the *Bradley,* in the tradition of great freighters, was performing in this way admirably.

By 5:00 P.M., both Mays and First Mate Elmer Fleming had, at some point, walked the entire length of the *Bradley* from front to back and neither one observed anything unusual. The ship was working the sea without a problem.

At 5:15 P.M., five minutes after sunset, the *Bradley* was holding a steady course, with the Beaver Island chain and Boulder Reef off the starboard bow (right front). Captain Bryan radioed in to Rogers City that he anticipated their arrival at 2:00 A.M. If they could inch their way a little bit farther, perhaps they could use those islands for some protection, as a windbreak against the fierce southwesterly blow. They were only about an hour or two away from safer waters. All they needed was a little more time. What they did not know was that time was rapidly running out for the *Bradley* and her ill-fated crew.

Mays and Gary Price, having completed the routine chore of pumping out the water that had accumulated after cleaning off the fine limestone left from the haul, decided to take a short break in the dunnage room, where ropes, ladders, and paint were stored. At around 5:30 P.M., suddenly, they heard a loud *thud,* coming from the ship's stern (rear), which was immediately followed by an eerie vibration that shook the entire ship. In his years on the lakes, Frank Mays had heard the strange creaking and groaning of these gentle giants, but this was different. Something was wrong. Seriously wrong.

CHAPTER FIVE

MAYDAY!

A round 5:30 P.M. Captain Bryan and his First Mate Elmer Fleming, both in the pilothouse, heard the very same deafening sound coming from behind them. Instinctively, they spun around, and were horrified by what they saw. Looking down the long deck toward the ship's stern, the string of deck lights still lit, a mariner's nightmare unfolded. The *Bradley*'s stern was sagging! Incredibly, she was breaking in half in the middle of Lake Michigan!

Mays and Price ran back to their cabin to get their life jackets, also grabbing Mays's wallet and watch. Then, taking giant steps, they leaped up the ladder leading to the main deck. They heard another resounding *thud* as the ship lunged up and then down, causing the stern to sag more. When they reached the main deck, Mays could not believe his eyes. A massive crack was opening up portside (left), near the number ten hatch. Mays looked in horror as the middle of the ship was humped about eight feet higher than the rapidly sagging stern, which was so much lower it was barely visible. Again and again the stern dipped down, then rose into view, and then disappeared again. Looking at the violent flexing and heaving of the long deck, Mays knew he could never make it all the way to his lifesaving station in the stern.

Both Captain Bryan and First Mate Fleming realized that the *Bradley* was going down. This was one of those "life and death" times when the captain and his crew go into survival mode. The captain ordered the engines stopped and sounded the "abandon ship" alarm on the ship's whistle: seven short whistles, followed by one long blast. Opinions differ on what exactly was said during the next frantic moments, but most agree that at the same time the captain was sounding the alarm, First Mate Fleming got on channel 51, the radio's emergency channel, and sent out this desperate and terrifying message to anyone who was listening: "Mayday! Mayday! Mayday! This is the *Carl D. Bradley*. We are breaking in two and sinking. We are twelve miles southwest of Gull Island. Any ships in the area, please come to our aid." In the background a voice, probably the captain's, was heard shouting, "Run! Grab your life jackets! Get your life jackets!"

As it turns out, lots of people heard the broadcast. Both commercial and amateur operators on land and sea were witness to the tragic human drama. Radio station WAD from Port Washington, Wisconsin, responded by verifying the ship's position as twelve miles southwest of Gull Island. But no one on the *Bradley* heard the radio's response, because just as Fleming ended his transmission, there were more *thuds*, and with each one the stern sagged lower and lower, raising the middle higher until, suddenly, she just broke into two gigantic 300-foot pieces! The wires and cables that ran through the ship snapped and sparked, flailing helplessly in the stormy winds. The radio went dead and most of the ship was plunged into darkness.

When Mays and Price headed to the front of the ship, Price joined about a half dozen men gathered around the captain. Mays, upon hearing First Mate Fleming shout over the roaring winds, "Someone get the life raft ready," ran over to the life raft that was behind the pilothouse.

Realizing that he did not have his life jacket in the pilothouse, Elmer Fleming ran, in total darkness, two decks below, down to his cabin, as precious seconds ticked off. Could the ship's bow (front) remain afloat long enough? When Fleming returned, in less than two minutes, the main deck was under water, and the ship's bow was sinking fast under their feet. The broken half of the hull was suspended precariously above water at a dramatically sharp angle as the tumultuous waves rocked the *Bradley* violently. Frank Mays, kneeling on the life raft, worked frantically to untie the raft and its oars. As Mays was doing this, Second Mate John Fogelsonger, after speaking briefly with the captain, tried to leap from the bow to the stern. Mays watched helplessly as the second mate fell into the ever-widening gap and disappeared, never to be seen again.

From the bow, Fleming could see three men on the stern trying to disengage one of the *Bradley*'s two lifeboats. Together, Erhardt Felax, Al Boehmer, and Paul Horn worked desperately to free the boat, but it got tangled up in the steel cable that held it. They grabbed a fire axe and frantically tried to chop the cable in half, but it was too thick. The lifeboat dangled uselessly as the stern moved sharply upward and began its downward descent, taking the men with it. Unaware of what was taking place at this very moment, the families would later be profoundly affected by their incalculable loss. Al's youngest son, Eric, was only eight months old and, like so many of the *Bradley* crewmembers' children, never had the chance to know his father.

The bow was listing to port (left) and Mays, who was still kneeling on the life raft, could see the captain and a small cluster of men gathered around him moving up to a higher point on the bow. The bow was going down faster than the stern, and its angle of entry was making it more difficult for the men to cling to life. They gripped the ship's railing, as the icy wind blew into them with its 65-mile-per-hour force. Then, in a split second, a mountainous wave hit the starboard side, thrusting the bow violently to the left, practically rolling it, and flinging all of the men on the bow into the 40° Fahrenheit water!

When the wave hit, Mays was hurled aboard the life raft, twenty feet into the air. When the raft came down, it was driven directly into the water, the steel-drum pontoons breaking the surface head on. Somehow, Mays was able to ride the raft through all of this, only to be knocked off when another wave tipped the craft. Shocked by the sudden icy immersion and pulled down deep, Mays, wearing his cork life jacket, quickly worked his way back up to the surface. Surrounded by the turbulent black water and thrashing two-story high waves, he could not see the raft. Mays, an excellent swimmer, did the only thing he could—he began to swim. On his first stroke his arm came down hard on an object. Miraculously, it was the raft! Though he had been totally disoriented when coming out of the water, the raft was apparently blown his way. Without a moment's hesitation, he grabbed the side rail, got a toehold on the pontoon, and climbed aboard the 8' × 10' platform. The raft was simple and primitive, consisting of steel drums that acted as pontoons, sandwiched between two wooden platforms. It was nothing fancy, to be sure, but it was his only hope for life.

Having been in the water for only a minute, Mays was catching his breath when he saw someone reaching for the raft and trying to climb up. Mays grabbed First Mate Elmer Fleming by his life-jacketed shoulders and dragged him onboard. When Mays was growing up in Rogers City, Fleming was his neighbor, living in an apartment across the street. What strange circumstances joined their lives in this way, sharing a raft in a raging November storm out on the middle of Lake Michigan!

In the darkness, the waves rose and crashed with deafening authority, as the winds howled relentlessly. The swirling, black waters lashed against and over the raft, spraying the men's faces with each icy blast. Unable to see above waves the size of houses, Mays and Fleming tried to catch a glimpse of someone, anyone who might be saved. They heard cries for help, haunting voices in the darkness swept away by the torrent or pulled beneath the waves, forever lost. Over and over, Elmer and Frank yelled as loud as they could, "We're over here. We have the raft." But the screaming wind and the roar of the sea drowned out their words. The oars had been lost when the ship rolled, leaving the two men very much alone and at the mercy of the lake.

Then, unexpectedly, they spotted Gary Strzelecki, a 21-year-old deck watch, who was able to make his way over to the raft. Elmer and Frank pulled him in and kept looking for others. During this time, the waves were knocking the little raft around like a piece of driftwood, as it bucked and rolled from side to side. But the three Rogers City men stayed on, and continued to call out to any others that might be within earshot. Blown uncontrollably in the raft, the men found themselves close to another crewman, Dennis Meredith, a 25-year-old deckhand. Dennis was the fourth man to board the raft, but he was in the worst shape. Wearing only very light clothing and barefoot, he was already suffering terribly from his exposure to the cold. His skin was grayish blue and, though barely conscious, he was not coherent. When the "abandon ship" whistle was sounded, he had been asleep in his bunk. Minutes before, Dennis was comfortable and safe, and now he was lying, shivering and unresponsive, on a flat board with three of his crewmates.

The four men continued to hear calls for help from those struggling to stay above water, but they were unable to maneuver the raft toward the faint voices that penetrated the darkness. Gary immediately recognized one voice as that of his brother-in-law, Ray Kowalski. Ray, a wheelsman, was in the pilothouse when that first terrifying *thud* was heard. Now he was a disembodied voice, calling out to the men. Gary was about to leave the raft and swim toward the voice to save his brother-in-law, but Elmer begged him to stay, trying to convince him that leaving the raft would mean certain death. After the next monster wave rolled past, Ray's voice was no longer heard. Gary was heartsick, staring blankly into the empty blackness, his eyes fixed on the spot where he last heard Ray's voice.

Mel Orr, a 35-year-old watchman, was the last crewmember they saw. Back home in Rogers City, his wife and three children were anxiously awaiting his return. When last seen, he was carried to the top of a wave, his hands over his head, before he disappeared behind it. And just that quickly, he was gone.

Although the bow had been dragged to Lake Michigan's depths, the stern somehow remained afloat. The aft cabin lights still twinkled in the darkness, and the men on the raft could only watch in horror and disbelief as the *Bradley*'s stern slowly rose, 250 feet in the air, angling itself vertically out of the water, with its giant propeller facing the stormy heavens. They could clearly see the starboard lifeboat dangling from the side, helpless and now useless. Then, when it was almost perpendicular to the water, the stern began to sink. When her mighty steam boilers made contact with Lake Michigan's freezing waters, a huge explosion of fire and smoke erupted. It was an explosion of such force and magnitude that even on these stormy seas, it could be seen for miles! The *Carl D. Bradley,* pride of the fleet, had fallen. At that moment, it was the largest ship in history to be lost on the Great Lakes.

The men on the raft looked in all directions. Nothing. They listened for any voices. No one. They were truly alone on the raft. The brutal storm had just taken a 639-foot ship and viciously torn it in half. What possible chance for survival could they have in these same treacherous waters aboard some wooden planks lashed to a couple of sealed oil drums? They had to have faith that the "Mayday" got through and help was on the way.

CHAPTER SIX

"ALL HANDS ARE LOST"

Four miles away, those aboard the German freighter *Christian Sartori* witnessed the flash of flame and smoke when the *Bradley*'s boiler exploded at about 5:40 P.M. At the same time, the *Bradley*'s image dropped off their radar. Even though they had not heard the *Bradley*'s "Mayday," the *Sartori* bravely rushed, at the height of the storm, in the direction of the explosion. The 254-foot ship and her courageous crew struggled against the high water and fierce winds. Captain Paul Mueller, a former German U-boat (submarine) officer, said that "it took us two hours to reach the spot where the *Bradley* went down," adding that the four-mile run would normally take only fifteen minutes.

Shortly after the *Bradley* went under, Fleming, the first mate and ranking officer, took charge. Knowing that the *Sartori* was somewhere in the vicinity, Fleming believed that it would undoubtedly be on its way and encouraged the men with this news. According to Mays, all four of the men were soon alert, focused on survival. He knew that their raft had a storage compartment. Opening it, he dug out three flares. When ignited, each flare would cast a lighted glow of red sparks. To light the flare, you had to remove a protective cap and then strike it against something, sort of like lighting a large match. With hands already numb from the cold, Fleming took one of the flares and ignited it. A warm, red light appeared, happily sparking its signal to any who could see. It certainly was not much, but it was all they had. There was nothing else to illuminate their position. No moon was visible that night, and the stars were masked by heavy cloud cover. When the *Bradley* vanished beneath the waves, the men were immersed in a darkness that was both physical and psychological.

When the flare extinguished itself, the men waited about a half hour before Fleming attempted to burn another flare. The second flare also ignited, providing light in the darkness and kindling prayers of rescue. for four desperate souls. Fleming saved the third flare for the first ship that became visible.

How those stranded men must have rejoiced at the first sign of the lights of the valiant *Sartori* as it rose and dipped in their direction in the teeth of gale-force winds and twenty-five-foot swells. Fleming was right. The *Sartori* was coming to the rescue. They were saved!

At 7:30 P.M., as the *Sartori* braved the treacherous water and slowly, ever so slowly, approached their position, Fleming decided it was time to ignite their last flare. Anxiously removing the cap, he struck it. Nothing. As the drenching spray washed over them and the wind's madness screamed in their heads, Fleming desperately struck the flare again and again. Nothing. The flare was dead. This could not be happening. The flare, like a match, had become too wet and would not ignite.

Upon reaching the scene of the disaster, the *Sartori* turned on its searchlight and scanned the water's surface, revealing the rising and crashing monster waves. Amazingly, the visibility was so poor due to the blinding sixty-mile-per-hour blowing that, although the raft was only about fifty yards from the *Sartori*, the men were not seen when the search beam passed over the water. The desperate men hollered as loud as they could, but to no avail. The ship was so close that the men felt that they could almost touch their would-be rescuers. Captain Mueller of the *Sartori* reported seeing only a raincoat and a tank floating in the water. Could that "tank" have been a glimpse of the life raft, or was it simply a remnant of the *Bradley*'s boiler explosion? No one can be certain.

Captain Mueller radioed in a somber message, stating everyone's worst fear: "I believe all hands are lost. No lifeboats visible." Loved ones had to confront the unimaginably painful possibility that Captain Mueller's words were true. A tragedy of such unspeakable magnitude simply could not happen to the tiny town of Rogers City. After all, since its founding in 1912, Bradley Transportation Company had never lost a ship. But the unthinkable was slowly becoming undeniable. There may be no survivors from the wreck of the S.S. *Carl D. Bradley*.

CHAPTER SEVEN

A PAINFUL UNCERTAINTY

The ominous words of the captain of the *Christian Sartori* put into motion a flurry of newspaper stories, coast to coast, that would end up on people's front porches the next morning. A November 19 headline in the *Los Angeles Times* read, "'No Lifeboats Visible': 35 Missing as Ship Splits in Two, Sinks." Sometimes the information was not entirely accurate, as was the case with the *Washington Post and Times Herald* headline of November 19: "Ship Sinks in Storm; No Trace of 37 Found."

Throughout the night, before the grim newspaper headlines appeared, some of the friends and families of the *Bradley's* crew made their way across the northern tip of Michigan's Lower Peninsula. They traveled from Rogers City to Charlevoix, Michigan, which was approximately fifty miles from where the *Bradley* was lost. They parked their cars on the beach of the great water and turned on their headlights to penetrate the darkness. It was there that they kept a solemn vigil, waiting for any news, hoping their prayers would be answered.

Among those waiting in Charlevoix was John Enos, the younger brother of Marty Enos, the 29-year-old stokerman on the *Bradley*. The six-foot-two, brown-haired Marty was well liked by everyone. A speedster who enjoyed the thrill of fast cars, Marty liked racing from his home in Cheboygan to Rogers City where he would board a freighter for another run. That night, John had planned to pick Marty up at 2:00 A.M. in Rogers City, but upon hearing the news of the ship's distress call, he instead rushed across the northern tier of the state to meet him in Charlevoix. Staring into the empty, endless blackness of the lake, John tried to remain hopeful that his big brother would arrive safely. Voices on the shore were drowned out by the deafening blow of angry winds. Alone with his thoughts, John recalled Marty's plans to marry his sweetheart, Frances, the sister of one his best friends. They were to get married in only a few days, so Marty just had to make it back. Tragically, his body would never be found.

Earlier that day, in Rogers City, it was windy but not at all stormy. In fact, the temperature was an almost balmy 66° Fahrenheit, unseasonably mild for November. Women hung their wash out on clotheslines and let the warm winds whip it dry. By nightfall, most of the townspeople heard the strong winds rattling their storm windows as they sat listening to their radios and televisions for any tidbits of information, anything that would confirm the men's safety or rescue. Together, the families and friends supported and consoled each other, hoping for the best, but bracing themselves for the worst. Everyone knew that there were lots of islands in the northern part of Lake Michigan. Maybe the men could seek refuge there. The painful uncertainty lasted all night in the homes of family and friends. They endured the long hours waiting for any news, reassuring each other, and imagining their unspoken worst fears.

Charlie Horn, brother of Paul, a 21-year-old oiler on the *Bradley*, was on Lake Huron the night the *Bradley* went down, working as second assistant engineer on the *John G. Munson*. The storm was not nearly as bad over near Lake Huron, and when the *Munson* docked in Rogers City, Charlie, knowing about the horrific storm on Lake Michigan, headed straight home for news of his brother. Before he made it home, a neighbor told Charlie's wife, Nancy, that he had heard on the television that the *Bradley* had sunk. Turning to Charlie's and Paul's mother, who was sitting right there in astonishment, he added, "But don't worry; the *Munson*'s standing by to help them." Their hope turned to horror when, just one hour later, Charlie walked through the back door. Why was he home so soon? Wasn't he on the *Munson,* the freighter that was going to save the *Bradley*? Confusion led to a mistaken assumption that the *Munson* was somewhere near the *Bradley*'s position, when in reality, the two vessels were on different lakes! Rumors and misinformation continued to swirl around the little town, reeling from the shock of the tragedy, making it difficult for loved ones to know what was happening.

In another home in Rogers City, Betty Kowalski, a young wife and mother, took her two small children, four and one, over to her parents' house. She was planning on having the kids spend the night with their grandma and grandpa while she went to meet her husband, Bob, who was expected to arrive on the *T. W. Robinson* later that evening. Suddenly, the phone rang. When she picked up the receiver, she heard the familiar voice of one of her friends ask her, "Did you hear the news?" Betty replied, "What news are you talking about?" Her friend answered, "One of our boats went down." When Betty responded, "Oh my God!" her friend promptly reassured her that both of their husbands were safe, adding that "It wasn't our boat. It was the *Bradley*." "My God," Betty cried out, "my brother's on there!"

Bernard "Benny" Schefke, Betty's 19-year-old brother, was indeed a porter on the *Bradley*. Shortly after the phone call, a neighbor came in with the same terrible news, but telling them not to worry because the Coast Guard was on its way. The neighbor tried to tell Benny's mother and sister that the men would be fine. But the words were hollow. Betty went to bed that night praying for her brother's safe return. After all, she told herself, he can swim, he can survive. But that unforgiving November night, the sea blew itself into a rage so relentlessly violent that it tore the mighty ship in two with its icy jaws.

While all of this was going on, the *Robinson* was tied up at Menominee, Wisconsin, because of the foul weather. The pilothouse heard Fleming's "Mayday!" transmission and word of the *Bradley*'s plight quickly spread. When Bob heard the news he turned to one of his shipmates, second engineer Lloyd Mays, and said, "You've got a brother on the *Bradley,* don't you?" Lloyd answered, "Yeah, my brother Frank's there. You have anyone on there?" And Bob answered, "My brother-in-law, Benny Schefke."

Throughout the long night, back in Rogers City, the families waited for news, any news about the *Bradley* and her crew of thirty-five. Back then, all of the telephones went through a central operator. There was no "call waiting" and no such thing as a cell phone. If you wanted to make a call, you picked up the receiver and asked the operator to connect you to the person you were calling. Because of this, it would have been very easy to tie up the lines of communication. Consequently, the residents of Rogers City were told to keep the telephone lines open and to make no calls except those that concerned the *Bradley.*

Waiting for news, any word at all, must have been torture for those families. But wait they did, usually as individual households and not as a group. After all, everyone wanted to be home if their phone rang. Alone with their thoughts and prayers, memories flooded back as the hours passed.

Charlie Horn thought about his little brother, Pete. Even though Paul was his name, everyone knew him as Pete. Recalling Pete one Christmas, all dressed up as Santa Claus for his nieces and nephews, brought a gentle smile to Charlie's face. That big, fluffy white beard hid Pete's youthful face, but it didn't fool the little children for even a minute. When they saw his dark eyebrows, they immediately called out, "Uncle Pete!" After Charlie had come in off the *Munson,* his family had gathered to celebrate the second birthday of his son, Tim. Little did Tim know that his birthday, November 18, would be forever linked to the great tragedy. The Horns would not have any news about Pete until 10:00 A.M. the next morning, nearly seventeen hours after the distress call.

The Schefke house, like the Horns', was quiet with anticipation, prayers, and concern for their loved one's well-being. Benny went to sea when he was only sixteen. It was in his blood, just like it was in his three brothers'. Happy-go-lucky and full of life, Benny loved his Model-A Ford with a fold-down rumble seat. His mom, on the other hand, was not so sure how much she liked that old car. Once after he took her out for a ride in it, she returned to the house out of breath and clearly scared, and said, "He took the turn so fast we were on just two wheels!" Of course, Benny, standing right behind her laughing, enjoyed the drive most of all. What could be better than taking your mom on a wild, nail-biting spin? As Benny's sister Betty thought about her brother, she knew that in four days, November 22, she would turn 21. What she could not have known was that on that very same day Benny, her little brother, would be buried.

While the families waited back in Rogers City, courageous search efforts were underway on the lake. At 6:20 P.M., shortly before the *Sartori*'s arrival at the scene of the disaster, the United States Coast Guard mobilized for a dangerous all-out search and rescue effort by air and sea. The Coast Guard station at Charlevoix launched the 180-foot cutter *Sundew,* captained by Lieutenant Commander Harold Muth. As the Charlevoix lift bridge blew its whistle to signal the cutter's departure, crowds gathered to watch the *Sundew* head out into the wild waters, knowing that only something major could make them to venture out into a life-threatening storm of this magnitude. Years later, in a television interview, Warren Toussaint, a hospital corpsman aboard the *Sundew,* said that "Our visibility was probably 100 feet because of waves, wind and rain and darkness." Recalling the cutter's terrifying crossing as it battled the lake on that night, Toussaint continued: "You know, people exaggerate things. I am not exaggerating. I know we had thirty- to forty-foot waves. . . . We took three 55° rolls. If you took one 60 we never would've come back. You stay flat and go down."

Just five minutes before the *Sundew*'s departure, a smaller (thirty-six-foot) rescue motor boat from the Charlevoix lifeboat station set out in an attempt to make the crossing. After only forty minutes, the little boat had to turn back because of the rough water.

On the other side of the lake, another Coast Guard ice-breaker, *Hollyhock,* left its station in Sturgeon Bay, Wisconsin, at 6:30 P.M. The Coast Guard Air Station at Traverse City, Michigan, was ordered to send one of its aircraft, a sea plane, to fly overhead and drop flares to improve visibility for the search vessels. The Traverse City base also had helicopters at the ready, but the weather was too dangerous and the winds were too strong to send them out at the time.

By 10:15 P.M. the *Elton Hoyt* and the *Robert C. Stanley,* two freighters, were also reported en route to the area; they arrived at about midnight. The *Sundew* arrived at the scene at 10:40 P.M., joining the *Sartori* in its search. The *Hollyhock* showed up at 2:30 A.M., and the ships engaged in a crisscross-pattern search. Throughout the night, the sea plane dropped a total of eighty-eight flares to light up the area, but they were quickly extinguished by the mountainous waves. The raft was nowhere to be seen, dragged away on an erratic course at the whim of the sea.

By about 8:00 A.M., Wednesday, November 19, the winds had calmed to thirty miles per hour but the lake's waves were still riding twenty to twenty-five feet. The slowing winds allowed for more air search. At this time, three Coast Guard helicopters from Traverse City, an Air Force Albatross search plane with amphibious (land and sea) capabilities, and a Navy PV2 plane all joined the search. Still, they found nothing.

Hope was beginning to dim. Despite their best efforts, the searchers could find no sign of life, not even a lifeboat.

■ CHAPTER EIGHT

AN ENDLESS NIGHT

The four men on the raft watched helplessly as the *Sartori* searched for them in the very waters that had, just hours before, consumed the *Bradley,* dragging her broken hull 365 feet beneath the raging turbulence. Disheartened that they were neither seen nor heard, the men knew that their only hope for survival was to cling to their raft, try to keep each other warm, and to stay awake. Elmer Fleming reminded them that since the *Sartori* knew about the wreck, the Coast Guard was probably on its way. Mays remembers adding these words of encouragement, "If we make it 'til daylight, we will be found." So that was what they faced. Somehow they had to help each other survive what would seem like an endless night.

The four men did whatever they could think of to stay warm and keep each other awake. They sang, talked, and counted. Elmer constantly nudged the boys, trying to make them talk and keep them awake. But they were exhausted. They huddled together and shared each other's warmth. Fleming even used his own body to try to shield Dennis Meredith from the lashing waves that crashed upon their tiny deck. Of the four, Dennis was perhaps most vulnerable to cold and hypothermia. Having been awakened in his bunk when the ship's alarm sounded, he was barefoot and wearing only a thin sweatshirt and pants. Unlike the other three men, he was not wearing a jacket, making it increasingly difficult for him to maintain his body temperature.

As gale-force winds blew the raft in a northeasterly direction, away from the site of the wreck, the four exhausted, shivering men began to encounter even larger waves, estimated by Mays at thirty and sometimes forty feet. The men were lifted, carried to the crest, and then slammed down into the wave's trough or dropped over the wave's backside from heights equivalent to a four-story building! It is no wonder that the raft flipped over repeatedly, dumping the men into the water and, each time, forcing them to muster the strength to pull themselves and one another back onto the raft.

Gary Strzelecki would sometimes warn the other men, who were lying chest down on the raft, using the slats between the planks for finger holds, when he saw big waves coming. How many hours could some-one sustain that position, gripping the slippery wooden boards, in drenched clothing, with cramping muscles and the threat of hypothermia as the body rapidly loses its heat? Elmer later recalled the harrowing ordeal of hanging on and then climbing back after being bucked off by the wild water: "I got so numb I was afraid I couldn't hang on to the raft with my hands. I swallowed a lot of water, but I always managed to get a good grip on the raft when I got back into it."

The first two times the raft flipped over, tossing all four men overboard, the first man able to scramble back on helped the next one and so on until all four men were back in the excruciatingly painful position of gripping the raft's planks. The third time the raft flipped over, Dennis Meredith was unable to get back on. According to Frank Mays, Dennis did not even attempt to pull himself up; he just hung on the edge of the raft. Gary, Elmer, and Frank grabbed his arms and tried to hoist him up, but they could not get him on board. Mays recalled that, during this time, Dennis never looked up or spoke. He was completely done in. Dennis was a year younger than Frank, and they had been classmates in school. They were not going to let go. Giving up on him was not an option. They would have to hold on to him until help arrived. Incredibly, they held on to their friend for hours with the hope that they would soon be rescued. Eventually, Frank realized that they were holding on to a body that was face-down in the water. Dennis had quietly slipped away. The moment that Gary and Frank released him, Dennis was gone. The lake had claimed another victim.

The men became quiet on the raft. What could anyone say? To Elmer, the boys on this raft were more than crewmates. He was forty-three years old, twenty-two years older than Gary, and more like a father to the boys than just the "ranking officer." They all took the loss hard and, lying there in silence, cast their thoughts adrift.

What could they be thinking at a time like this? Gary Strzelecki, just twenty-one, was married to Ann, who was twenty years old. Together they had begun their little family with Benjamin, their nine-month-old son. During the off-season, they would have a terrific birthday party for him. His first birthday celebration would be a day to remember. Gary's heart went out to his sister, Mavis, whose husband, Ray Kowalski, was lost. He had heard Ray's voice amid the chaos of wind and water. But what could he have done? And what would he say to her and her four children? And then there were his parents and grandparents, and everyone else in Rogers City. His dad was hoping Gary might join him in an electrical contracting business. Right now, that plan seemed so far off.

As the seaman with the most experience, Elmer Fleming knew that he had to keep their hopes and spirits up. But now only three remained. By all accounts, Elmer was a respected sailor and an excellent navigator. He pinpointed their location almost exactly when he radioed in the distress call. Strong both physically and emotionally, Elmer would have to be a rock for these boys to rely on. He was a quiet, serious man, and because of this, people sometimes saw him as stern. But when he settled down over a cup of coffee with friends, he would smile and show a gentler side. His strong jaw line revealed a character of great tenacity and determination.

As he lay on that raft, freezing, weak, and helpless, Elmer's thoughts returned to his wife, Mary and their 15-year-old son, Douglas. How he loved them. These thoughts brought on a sense of comfort and a temporary escape. Elmer rose through the ranks and had always wanted to be a captain. Was this how it would all end? He had to be strong, for himself and for those boys sharing the raft.

Perhaps Frank was right. Hang on until first light. They would certainly be rescued. Was it possible that anyone else could have survived? Were they the only ones remaining? In all Elmer's years at sea, he had seen big water before, having survived the great Armistice Day Storm of 1940 aboard the *T. W. Robinson*. But he never would have imagined himself where he now was, completely at the mercy of the haunting winds and the raging waters, on this the blackest of November nights.

For a brief moment, it could have been summertime. Frank Mays's thoughts drifted back in time to a warm, July afternoon. His father fished from a lakeshore, while Frank pushed the top of a picnic table out to the middle of the lake and used it for diving. What a fine swimmer he was! He could swim across a good-sized lake and dive forty feet below its surface. Or perhaps his memories wandered to a cold, winter morning, when he was just a little boy on his way to school. While he was crossing a forbidden patch of ice on Lake Huron, it suddenly gave way. Down he fell, maybe twelve feet. When he bobbed to the surface, he pulled himself up on the edge of the ice hole and ran home. After changing his clothes, he went to school, never telling his mom about the incident.

Like everyone else who grew up in Rogers City, Frank was most at home when he was close to big water. Unlike their dad, who did not much like sailing, Frank's two brothers signed on to ships on the Great Lakes at a very young age. His oldest brother, Harry, began his maritime life at sixteen, when most teenagers were thinking about going to dances, getting a driver's license, or playing football. And then there was Lloyd, who was just two years older than Frank. Lloyd started sailing during the summers while still in high school and, like so many other boys in Rogers City, ended up making a career sailing for Bradley Transportation. On the night of the eighteenth, Lloyd got the news of the

Bradley while aboard the *Robinson,* tied up in dock at Menominee in Lake Michigan's Green Bay.

Frank's path to the sea would be almost as direct as that of his brothers. Two days after graduating from high school, he got hired on his first freighter as a deckhand. Following this, he served a four-year stint in the Navy, where he met Marlys Bush, the niece of a Navy friend. Frank and Marlys were married while he was still in the Navy, and by the time he got out, the young couple had become a small family with the arrival of their firstborn, Michael. They decided to move to Iowa, Marlys' home state. Many miles from the Great Lakes, Frank found himself in a variety of jobs, including working in a machine shop and driving a delivery truck. Their little family grew, with the addition of another son, Mark. Frank found that the land-locked cornfields of Iowa were no place for someone who loved the lakes and needed to sail. The family packed up their belongings and moved back to Rogers City, where Frank once again found himself on board the mighty freighters.

Frank's meandering thoughts transported him to the present. In his mind he could see Marlys and the boys, four-year-old Michael and two-year-old Mark. And lovingly he could visualize yet another sweet, little face. Just one short month before, Marlys had given birth to little Frank, their third son. If he could survive this stormy nightmare, in just five days he would celebrate his twenty-seventh birthday with his family.

A chilling spray abruptly slapped Frank out of his dreamy reverie. He had to focus on surviving this night. Frank later revealed that, "There was never any doubt in my mind that someone would find us if we could last through the night. I prayed a lot, and I got pretty scared when I found that there was ice forming on my hair and crusted on my jacket, but I still felt that if we could make it 'til daylight we'd be okay." Although the men continued to have faith in their eventual rescue, the night was long and cold, and they were tossed into the water at least one more time before a faint blush of light on the horizon became visible.

It must have been about 7:30 A.M. when Frank looked over at Elmer and was relieved to see that he was still awake. But something was wrong with Gary. He was not making eye contact and was unresponsive when they tried to talk to him. Without warning, Gary made his way on his hands and knees to the edge of the raft as if he was going to drop into the water and swim away. Terrified at the thought, Elmer and Frank acted quickly, holding Gary as firmly as they could, but it was no use. Gary ripped himself from them, rolled into the water, and swam away! The raft was their only hope, and Gary, confused and suffering from hypothermia, abandoned it. Elmer and Frank were helpless to save him. Following him into the water would have cost them their lives. Suffering from the effects of hypothermia, painful muscle cramps, penetrating chills, and complete exhaustion, a rescue attempt was not possible.

Now that there were just the two of them, Frank and Elmer wondered, if by some miracle they were to survive, how they would cope with such staggering loss. And the loss went far beyond just the two of them. How would a whole town conquer the immeasurable grief? In times of adversity, these questions plumb the depths of the human soul.

Daylight was breaking, and the little raft continued to be pulled by the currents. As Frank strained his eyes against the dim horizon, he could just barely make out what looked like an island. Elmer told Frank that he thought it was High Island, one of the uninhabited islands that is part of the Beaver Island chain. Slowly, as the minutes ticked away, the raft drew closer to the land. Mays estimated that they were within sixty yards when the currents played the cruelest trick imaginable. The raft was pulled *away* from the island's shore. Though the temptation to swim the distance must have been hard to resist, both men knew that they were safest aboard the raft. As the light inched its way across the glistening waves, Elmer Fleming and Frank Mays were thinking the same thought. With the coming light, rescue could not be far away.

CHAPTER NINE

RESCUE!

There was a hint of sunlight on Wednesday morning, November 19, about 8:00 A.M. The winds had slowed somewhat, allowing three Coast Guard helicopters, an Air Force plane, and a Navy plane to join the search. The Coast Guard Cutters *Sundew* and *Hollyhock,* who had been battling the storm all night, were still searching. After combing the area for more than twelve hours, all of the commercial and military vessels involved came up with the same result: No luck. They found no sign of survivors; not a single body had been recovered.

The brave and now exhausted crew of the *Sundew* refused to give up, continuing to make their routine passes in the vicinity of Gull Island and High Island to the northeast. It was 8:25 A.M. when a lookout in the *Sundew*'s wheelhouse thought that he saw something straight ahead. The captain of the *Sundew,* Lieutenant Commander Muth, grabbed his binoculars and tried to get a fix on the object. A brief glimpse showed something that looked like a small boat. Could it be a lifeboat? It quickly disappeared from sight in the deep trough of a twenty-five-foot wave. Then it rose up again. It was a raft with two men! Although the waves were still high, the winds were now thirty miles per hour, and the *Sundew* was able to maneuver its way alongside the raft in just eight minutes. Four minutes later, at 8:37 A.M., Elmer Fleming and Frank Mays were rescued and safely aboard the *Sundew*. Lieutenant Commander Muth reported the good news and radioed in their position as 5.25 miles northeast of Gull Island. The erratic, storm-tossed journey had carried Fleming and Mays twenty miles from where the *Bradley* sank.

After fifteen hours, the terrible ordeal endured by Frank Mays and Elmer Fleming had finally come to an end. So weak were the men, they could not even lift their arms to grab the line that the *Sundew* threw to them. Hungry, shivering, and exhausted beyond description, both men were wrapped in warm wool blankets when they made it on board. Without hesitation, both Frank and Elmer insisted that they be allowed to remain on board for the search of their fellow crewmen rather than be taken directly back to Charlevoix. It was an amazing testament of courage and unselfishness that meant many more hours at sea, but both men were concerned about their shipmates and wanted to be there if any others should be rescued.

At 9:28 A.M., they came alongside one of the *Bradley*'s lifeboats, over-turned and unused. It was found about two miles from Mays and Fleming's life raft. Presumably, it was the same starboard lifeboat that Elmer Fleming observed the three men struggling to deploy and that was seen dangling from the *Bradley*'s stern when she vanished, making her tragic descent. As the *Sundew* was making its approach to get the lifeboat, a helicopter reported two bodies floating about 400 yards north of Gull Island. Then, a third body was spotted, and by 10:10 A.M., Coast Guard helicopters had reported a total of seven bodies sighted. The *Sundew* had to begin the grisly task of bringing the dead aboard. Receiving help from her sister boat, the *Hollyhock,* the *Sundew* and some forty-foot patrol boats maneuvered the rough waters, looking for the bodies that were sighted. By midday, the *Sundew* had recovered eight bodies, the *Hollyhock* had brought five bodies aboard, and the Beaver Island patrol had four bodies on board. At this point, there were seventeen victims recovered thus far and only the two survivors.

It was a little after noon when the Captain of the *Sundew* was advised by Warren Toussaint, the medic on board, that Frank and Elmer's temperatures were rising, and it would be wise to get them back to Charlevoix as soon as possible to avoid the risk of pneumonia. Despite their desire to stay with the search, it was more important to get these men back safely on dry land where they could be transported to a hospital and a doctor's care.

Lieutenant Commander Muth had turned the search over to the *Hollyhock* and was about to head back when a message crackled over the radio. A German freighter, *TransOntario,* was reporting that they had seen a body close to the west shore of High Island. The following message was scribbled in Lieutenant Commander Muth's ship's log (1:14 P.M., November 19, 1958): "German M/V *TransOntario* called and asked for doctor to be sent to them, body they picked up may have some life in it." This message put into motion one of the most intriguing and heroic rescue attempts imaginable. The body was that of young Gary Strzelecki who, weakened and confused, had rolled himself off the raft and swum away into the misty fog of early dawn. After surviving fourteen brutally cold hours, he swam away from the raft just one hour before his friends were finally found and rescued.

But now, according to the message, there appeared to be a glimmer of hope. Was there really a way for Gary to survive all of this? No time was wasted. He needed medical attention immediately, and the nearest doctor was on Beaver Island. The largest in a chain of mostly uninhabited islands, Beaver Island had at the time a population of only about 300. And they had only one doctor: Dr. Frank E. Luton. The quickest way to transport Dr. Luton to the *TransOntario*'s deck would be by helicopter. But that was not the only problem. The doctor would have to be lowered in a harness, dangling from the helicopter in thirty-mile-per-hour winds. Then, he would have to make it all the way down to the deck of the ship, which was pitching and rolling in rough water. To complicate things even further, Dr. Luton was seventy-nine years old!

It is said that we gain strength through adversity. Such strength can reveal a depth of character and commitment to others that might otherwise go unnoticed and, therefore, unrecognized. Perhaps the true hero is the person who unselfishly helps others without expecting anything in return. When Dr. Luton accepted the mission to help the young sailor, he did so without any concern for his own safety. Like the brave men who battled the high seas all night in search of survivors, Dr. Luton showed a courage that is rare.

The helicopter pilot, Lieutenant James Sigman, picked up the doctor on Beaver Island and flew him to the waiting freighter. As they hovered over the vessel and prepared Dr. Luton to be lowered on to the deck, the *TransOntario* radioed the message that the body no longer showed signs of life.

By the end of the day, November 19, the bodies of eighteen of the *Bradley*'s crew had been recovered; all were wearing life jackets. Back in Rogers City, the children of some of the crewmen had gone to school, and as the lifeless bodies of their fathers were recovered from the lake, one by one the children were informed of the horrible news. The *Trans-Ontario* carried Gary Strzelecki's body to Milwaukee, where it was then flown to his home in Rogers City. The remaining seventeen bodies were taken to the Charlevoix City Hall, which was temporarily converted into a makeshift morgue so that families could identify their loved ones.

In the days that followed, searches by land and water continued,, but no other victims were found. All that was found were some life jackets that had been laced, an indication that they might have been worn but slipped off of the bodies. The bodies of the fifteen remaining crewmen, including Captain Roland Bryan and Dennis Meredith (the fourth man on the raft), were never recovered, and were listed by the Coast Guard as "missing and presumed dead."

Elmer Fleming and Frank Mays, the *Bradley*'s only survivors, were transported by ambulance to a hospital where they recuperated for a few days and tried to get some much-needed rest. After all, they had not slept for about thirty hours! Considering what these men had been through, it was truly remarkable that they were in such good shape, suffering mainly from shock and exposure. Mays admitted, "I was never so cold in my life." And there was good reason. The temperature that night on the lake was dangerously low and, due to sixty-five-mile-per-hour winds, cut right to the bone. Yet neither man showed signs of frostbite. Perhaps Frank and Elmer's doctor summed it up best, describing their survival as "an amazing piece of human endurance."

CHAPTER TEN

"A FUNERAL ON EVERY STREET"

The reality was just beginning to sink in. Thirty-three men had lost their lives in one of the worst maritime disasters of the century. And twenty-three of them came from Rogers City, a town of less than 3,800 people. The community now had to brace itself for the arrival from Charlevoix of those bodies recovered from the *Bradley* tragedy. In fact, of the eighteen bodies recovered, fifteen were coming home to Rogers City or nearby Onaway. On November 20, in the *Detroit Free Press,* Eleanor Tulgetske, whose husband Earl was lost on the *Bradley,* poignantly observed that she always knew her town lived by the ships, but now they were dying by them. The young mother of four uttered a sentiment that rang true for many.

Up to this point, the recovered victims' bodies had been identified by loved ones. Strange though it may seem, however, one of the widows was not allowed to legally identify the body of her own husband—Bill Elliott, a repairman on the *Bradley.* Bill's wife, Sandra, the mother of two small children, was just twenty years old and considered a minor.

With each day that passed, things did not get any easier for the surviving families. The painful ordeal continued, as preparations were made for funerals, memorial services, and an influx of friends and relatives that would practically double the little town's population.

The whole country and particularly the state of Michigan mourned the loss, showing an outpouring of sympathy for the families. It is difficult to understand the burden that Rogers City had to bear, and, as is often the case in times of tragedy, a sense of helplessness makes it hard to know what to say. With this in mind, in a November 19 editorial, the *Detroit Free Press* noted: "The loss falls shockingly heavy on Rogers City, the home port of the *Bradley* and the majority of her crew. There are no words of solace which can comfort the hearts of the families of the sailors who will not come home again." The wives of those who were safely aboard other ships at the time tried to console the grief-stricken widows of the *Bradley*. In a bittersweet moment, Mary Fleming, wife of survivor Elmer Fleming, said, "I'm happy my husband is safe, but I can't be completely happy because so many others are dead or still missing."

In the days immediately following the disaster, an eerie silence settled over the tiny maritime community. Charlie Horn, who lost his younger brother, recalled that he had never seen a town so quiet. To him it seemed like the whole town was in shock, because the tragedy struck so suddenly, without warning. A somber and agonizing reality set in when they started bringing in the bodies, and the grieving town tried to comprehend a loss of staggering proportions.

Everyone had expected that the *Bradley* would arrive and drop anchor at 2:00 A.M., signaling the beginning of the off season. It would be a good time, a happy time, a time for family. Thanksgiving was almost upon them, and then Christmas and New Year's. There would be celebrations, gifts, and parties. But now everything had changed. It was all so chaotic and confusing. How could this be happening? A numbing sense of disbelief was soon displaced by anger and helplessness. How would these young mothers explain to the children that their fathers were never coming home again? Consumed by an overwhelming emptiness left by the loss of their loved ones, the families did the only thing they could—prepare for funeral services.

On Friday, November 21, coffins containing the bodies of all of the hometown victims were placed in the Rogers City High School gymnasium. They remained there all day, allowing friends and relatives a peaceful moment for meditation and prayer. The next day, Saturday, was declared an official day of mourning by Rogers City Mayor Kenneth P. Vogelheim. All businesses would be closed. In an official proclamation, he declared that each year, November 18 would be dedicated to the memory of those lost on the *Bradley*.

Saturday and Sunday were a weekend of funeral services for all of Rogers City and neighboring Onaway. Mayor Vogelheim later noted that "There was literally a funeral on every street. The town just couldn't hold all the grief." Funeral and memorial services were held at churches of various denominations—Catholic, Presbyterian, and Lutheran. The largest mass funeral was held on Saturday, at St. Ignatius Catholic Church, for nine crewmembers. Photographs depict the packed sanctuary with all nine caskets lined up, single file, down the center aisle of the church. It is said that 2,000 people attended, filling the church and spilling over to the church school auditorium, and even out on to the street.

Those nine caskets included the bodies of Gary Strzelecki and his brother-in-law Ray Kowalski, whose voice Gary heard above the howling winds of that horrible storm. Gary had desperately wanted to leave the raft to save Ray but the voice went silent. Now both were gone, and their loss left five children fatherless. Frank Mays's cousin and good friend, Alva Budnick, was also in one of the caskets that filled the aisle at St. Ignatius. Joe Krawczak, husband and father of six, was in the line of nine caskets, too. And there was Benny Schefke, who at nineteen was one of three teenagers who had signed on to the *Bradley*. The other two teenagers, James Selke (18) and Dennis Joppich (19), both from Rogers City, were never found.

The funerals continued on Saturday for Pete Horn and Paul Heller at St. John's Lutheran Church. When the *Bradley* was lost, Pete's brother, Charlie, was weathering a storm aboard the *Munson* on Lake Huron before docking that night in Rogers City. Soon he had the painful task of identifying his 21-year-old younger brother in the makeshift morgue in

Charlevoix. For the Heller family, this was the third family loss in seven months; two of Paul's brothers had died earlier in the year.

Services for Cleland Gager and Gary Price, both of nearby Onaway, were held on Sunday. On November 17, Cleland Gager had just celebrated his thirtieth birthday aboard the *Bradley*. The very next day he was gone. Less than a week later, his wife and three children were attending his funeral. Gary Price was the 21-year-old deckhand who was below deck with Frank Mays when the terrifying *thud* was first heard. Just minutes later, as Frank tried to prepare the life raft, Gary joined others who were gathered around the captain. That was the last time Frank saw him.

In the end, the *Bradley*'s human casualties exceeded the thirty-three men lost. With the Thanksgiving holiday rapidly approaching, families in Rogers City had little to celebrate. Twenty-three wives had become widows and fifty-three children were now fatherless.

CHAPTER ELEVEN

WHAT HAPPENED?

The funerals had concluded and the loved ones buried. It was time for the families to try to piece their lives back together. But closure did not come easy. There were still many unanswered questions. Why was the *Bradley* even out on the lake that night, when eight other ships had dropped anchor in safe harbor? What condition was she in? After all, the ship had been scheduled during winter lay-up for work totaling more than $800,000. Was she really seaworthy? How much of the tragedy could be due to the storm and how much to the ship's structural weaknesses? Was all the safety equipment on board adequate, including life jackets, signal flares, and mechanisms for deploying lifeboats? One of the worst Great Lakes maritime disasters had just occurred, and the families believed that they deserved answers. They hoped that a thorough Coast Guard investigation would provide some much-sought-after insight into the cause of this tragedy.

In the spring of 1959, after the ice of Lake Michigan broke up, the U.S. Army Corps of Engineers, aided by sonar equipment aboard the *MS Williams,* was able to locate the ship's exact position as well as get a sense of its size and shape. It was reported that the ship was lying five miles northwest of Boulder Reef, just south of Gull Island at depths between 360 and 370 feet.

The wreck site was revisited that same year when U.S. Steel Corporation, the *Bradley*'s owners since 1952, hired the Los Angeles-based Global Marine Exploration Company. Contrary to the eyewitness accounts of Mays and Fleming, the company, using underwater television equipment, concluded "that the vessel lay in one piece." One can only imagine the frustration felt by Mays and Fleming when their accounts were challenged in this way. However, neither man wavered in his claim that the *Bradley* broke in two—after all, they saw it happen!

Within days of the accident, the Coast Guard began its investigation concerning why the *Bradley* went down, proposing recommendations for improved shipping safety. It was conducted by a four-man board chaired by Rear Admiral Joseph Kerrins. To determine the cause of the disaster, the board focused on four general areas. First, they considered whether any physical encounters might have occurred on this voyage (such as a brush with Boulder Reef). They also looked into structural concerns (problems linked to the ship's condition). A third issue could be designated "Act of God" (matters relating to the severity of the storm). Finally, there was the captain's culpability: Was Captain Bryan at fault for attempting to ride out the storm?

The board concluded that the ship did not strike Boulder Reef, noting that if the *Bradley* been damaged by the reef, she could not have traveled the five-mile distance to the place where her journey ended. They determined that the ship broke in two because of "excessive hogging stresses." Hogging refers to the phenomenon that occurs when high waves under a freighter actually raise the middle of the ship, causing it to "hump" or arch upward. Although the *Bradley*'s hull was designed to allow for a certain amount of flexibility, hogging places incredible stress on a ship and can trigger a crack that could lead to the metal snapping in two.

Failure due to hogging stresses would be more likely if the metal hull were weakened due to rust or hairline fractures. The rising motion of the waves repeatedly bends the middle up and when the waves fall, the hull begins to sag. Imagine taking a piece of metal and continually bending it back and forth, working it until a crease appears and a crack opens. Hogging stresses from the lake could have had that effect on the *Bradley*. The humping upward of the ship's middle was observed by Mays, who recalled that the stern would appear and then disappear as the middle raised itself approximately eight feet above the aft section. Some hogging in unusually heavy seas does not necessarily suggest a problem with a ship's structure since this can damage even a healthy hull.

The board noted the existence of hairline fractures on the *Bradley*'s bottom, but they were unsure whether this could in any way be linked to her breaking up. In fact, the board determined that no structural problems contributed to the casualty, including those caused by the two unreported mishaps in Cedarville. Still, Captain Bryan's own words reflected concern about the ship's structural integrity when he wrote, just ten days before she sank, that the *Bradley* was "getting pretty ripe for too much weather." Nevertheless, it was the board's conclusion that she was seaworthy when she left Gary on the evening of November 17.

Rather than focus on the vessel's structural integrity, the board turned its attention to the storm itself and Captain Roland Bryan's decision to depart, despite knowing the severe storm forecasts and gale warnings. The board made special note that this particular storm had been "described by various shipmasters as the most severe they have encountered." The report also emphasized the historical hazards linked to November sailings, citing that "between 1900 and 1950, over one-third of the vessels lost by foundering were lost during November, and over one-half of all strandings occurred in November."

Given all of this, the board determined that Captain Bryan, in his "zealous desire" to follow his schedule, "exercised poor judgment" when he decided to leave the protection of the Wisconsin shoreline and head toward Lansing Shoal, across Lake Michigan. In what may have been a veiled reference to the eight ships that dropped anchor in safe harbors that night, the board said the following of Captain Bryan: "he gave less attention to the dangers of the existing weather than might be expected of a prudent mariner." The board concluded that it was Captain Bryan's judgment, rather than the ship's structural integrity, that raised the most serious concerns.

Then something rather unusual happened. On July 7, 1958, Vice Admiral A. C. Richmond submitted his own report, a "Commandant's Action," in response to the Coast Guard Marine Board's investigation. His conclusions proved to be quite different from those of the board.

Although he agreed that hogging stresses led to the ship's break up, Vice Admiral Richmond disagreed with the board's contention that Captain Bryan used poor judgment and acted imprudently. He pointed out that the ship had by all accounts been riding smoothly in heavy seas, right up to the very moment of the first *thud*.

Why then was the *Bradley* lost? Other than citing the captain's role in all of this, the board "offered no other conclusions as to the possible cause of this disaster." By contrast, Richmond speculated that the problem might be linked to the *Bradley*'s structural weaknesses. The hairline cracks, unreported groundings at Cedarville, and need for a completely new cargo hold, in Richmond's words, raise "the obvious question as to the general condition of the vessel's structure." While acknowledging the severity of the weather on that night, Richmond maintained that the *Bradley* should have "easily" been able to survive the storm. This led Richmond to conclude that the *Bradley* had "developed an undetected structural weakness or defect." So the board pointed its finger at Captain Bryan and his ill-fated decision to weather the storm, and Richmond blamed the *Bradley*'s structural weaknesses.

Both the Coast Guard Marine Board and Vice Admiral Richmond did, however, find some common ground regarding safety recommendations. When the *Bradley* went down, the angle of the sinking stern made it almost impossible for the men to deploy the lifeboats. The Coast Guard Marine Board recommended mechanical changes in the way lifeboats are disengaged and launched. Not surprisingly, the board cited that a second life raft should also be mandatory on Great Lakes cargo ships. The great advantage to a life raft is that its top and bottom are identical, giving it the ability to land right side up, no matter how many times or ways it is overturned. A lifeboat, on the other hand, can get swamped in heavy seas. Considering that the life raft was integral to the survival of Mays and Fleming, it made sense that the Coast Guard would recognize its life-saving value.

The need for different types of signal flares was also cited. The board recommended that each lifeboat and life raft include "red, parachute-type flare" signals and equipment for firing them skyward. In fact, they said at least six should be stored on each lifeboat and raft. The *Bradley*'s raft had only three manually lit flares, and of these, only two ignited. A flare gun would send a more visible signal, and a parachute flare would probably be seen from a greater distance.

One of the most important recommendations pertained to the life jackets issued to the crew of the *Bradley*. The jackets were made of cork and canvas and, although they were Coast Guard–approved, they were very outdated. One of the biggest problems associated with the jackets was that they had no crotch strap, making it all too easy for them to slip off. The other problem was that they did not have a collar to support the neck, keeping the head out of the water. The board suggested that crews be equipped with life jackets that have both of these features. Nevertheless, neither of these improvements would have helped the crew of the *Bradley*. No one could have survived more than a few minutes in the bone-chilling waters of Lake Michigan on that night.

Clearly, the families of those lost on the *Bradley* did not believe that their loved ones should have been placed in harm's way on that dreadful night. For them, there could be only one inescapable conclusion: The *Carl D. Bradley* should not have been out on Lake Michigan on November 18. Unable to achieve closure from the incident, the hearings, and the differing explanations, the families filed a lawsuit against U.S. Steel, seeking damages of $16,490,000. In August 1960 the families of the crew were awarded a settlement of $1,250,000. Each family received between $2,808 and $73,390, depending on the age of a crewmember, his years of service, how many children he had. The *Detroit Times* established the *Carl D. Bradley* Ship Disaster Children's Fund, which raised $154,000 that was used to establish a group health insurance policy for the *Bradley* widows and their children.

After the initial media attention faded and the public fascination burned itself out, the tragedy of the *Bradley,* unfortunately, sank into obscurity. As is often the case, people can be fickle and easily distracted. In the years that followed, songs of the ill-fated voyage were not sung, stories of the record-breaking ship were not told, and the legend of the *Carl D. Bradley* vanished as quickly as the ship did on that terrible November night. Life went on for the rest of the country, but for Rogers City and the widows and their children, life would be forever changed. Fathers and future grandfathers were lost not only to the sea but also to future generations. Their story remained untold.

CHAPTER TWELVE

EPILOGUE

After the *Bradley* tragedy, life in Rogers City was slow to return to normal. However, lives had to go on, sailors had to ship out, and business in the nautical city resumed without incident. That is, until May 7, 1965, when tragedy once again struck the harbor town.

In a thick, dense fog in the Straits of Mackinac, the waters separating Lake Michigan and Lake Huron, the *Cedarville* and the *Topdalsfjord,* a Norwegian freighter, attempted to pass each other. The captain of the *Cedarville* made a right turn, thinking that this would enable them to pass on each other's left side, and the *Topdalsfjord* rammed her, ripping a huge gash. If the *Cedarville*'s captain had only sailed straight, without turning in front of the Norwegian vessel, they would have passed on each other's right side without a problem. The collision should never have happened, since both ships were equipped with radar. A Coast Guard investigation concluded that the *Cedarville*'s captain was traveling too fast for the foggy conditions, and that his actions cost ten men, nine of whom were from Rogers City, their lives.

On August 9, 1987, a memorial was established in Rogers City's Lakeside Park, on the shores of Lake Huron. It was dedicated to the forty-three men who lost their lives on the *Bradley* and the *Cedarville.*

One of the *Bradley*'s two survivors, Elmer Fleming, continued to sail, realizing his dream of becoming captain. Shortly after the *Bradley* tragedy, Fleming was named captain on the *W. F. White*, and he eventually retired as captain of the *Cedarville*, the same ship that later sank in the Straits of Mackinac. In 1969 he died of a heart attack, leaving Frank Mays as the only living survivor of the *Bradley*.

Unlike Fleming, Frank Mays never returned to sailing, though he did continue working for Bradley Transportation for a while. After that, he worked for a lumber company and then took a job with a cement company in Charlevoix, Michigan. They transferred him to Pennsylvania and then to Florida, where Frank retired.

In August 1995 Mays was offered a rare opportunity to visit the *Bradley* wreck site. As a passenger in a mini-submarine, he was able to actually land on the *Bradley*'s deck, a place where Mays had not been for nearly thirty-eight years! Although the muddy waters interfered with the visibility, as the submarine moved slowly past the hull, huge letters emblazoned across the right side of the stern appeared: Carl D. Bradley. After nearly half an hour on Lake Michigan's bottom, they ascended, without seeing both halves of the ship.

Nevertheless, Mays achieved complete satisfaction two years later, when he revisited the wreck site aboard a boat equipped with a Remote Operated Vehicle (ROV). A ROV is a self-propelled, freely moving apparatus that is capable of sending high-tech video images to monitors on board the boat. Mays was able to view the wreck of the *Bradley* on the monitors as the ROV maneuvered its way around the ship. And he saw what he had always known: The *Bradley* lay on the bottom in *two* pieces, separated by about 120 feet. When Global Marine Exploration Company, hired by U.S. Steel back in 1959, had reported that "the object was in one piece," they cast doubt on Frank Mays and Elmer Fleming's eyewitness accounts that the ship had literally broken in two. Nearly forty years later, Mays had his moment of vindication. In his words, "I saw it in two pieces on the surface, and now I've seen it in two pieces on the bottom of Lake Michigan."

Sometimes it takes a tragedy of unspeakable horror to remind us of the obvious. These ships, while governed by the mundane, economic demands of business, operate at the mercy of nature. They carry something far more valuable than stone and ore. We would do well to remember that there is no more precious cargo than the fathers and husbands, brothers and sons, uncles and grandfathers on board these mighty ships. If there is a lesson to be gleaned from any of this perhaps it is this: It would be better to err on the side of safety, rather than risk the lives of a crew in a treacherous gale.

That hellish November storm left twenty-three women widowed and fifty-three children without their fathers. It erased the future from three teenage crewmembers and several boys in their early twenties—their future marriages and children and grandchildren.

To this day, the surviving families often liken the human toll to a war-time loss. The suddenness of the tragedy, the youthfulness of so many of its victims, and the violence of the attack are all silent reminders of this war where the enemy was not man, but rather nature. This wasn't a fight for ideology, power, or dominion. It was a struggle for life itself. And though it may be hard to understand, the families of the eighteen men whose bodies were recovered expressed comfort in knowing that at least their loved ones could be buried. They could now visit the gravesites and achieve some small measure of closure. The other fifteen men, however, remained forever lost to the depths of the lake, much like those "missing in action" whose caskets never returned from war.

For the tiny community of Rogers City, life would never again be the same. The town would move forward, but it would never forget the disaster—nor should it. The *Carl D. Bradley* tragedy is a tale of unimaginable loss and remarkable courage. Remembering the men of the *Bradley* is to honor their lives.

CREW LIST

CREW	RANK	AGE	RESIDENCE
Roland Bryan	Captain	52	Loudonville, N.Y.
Elmer Fleming*	First Mate	43	Rogers City, Mich.
John Fogelsonger	Second Mate	31	St. Ignace, Mich.
Carl Bartell†	Third Mate	25	Rogers City, Mich.
Raymond Buehler	Chief Engineer	59	Lakewood, Ohio
John Bauers	First Asst. Engineer	30	Rogers City, Mich.
Alfred Boehmer†	Second Asst. Engineer	32	Rogers City, Mich.
Keith Schular	Third Asst. Engineer	36	Rogers City, Mich.
Douglas Bellmore	Porter	34	Onaway, Mich.
Duane Berg	Deckhand	25	Rogers City, Mich.
Richard Book†	Deckwatchman	26	Portsmouth, Iowa
Alva Budnick†	Watchman	26	Rogers City, Mich.
William Elliott†	Repairman	26	Rogers City, Mich.
Clyde "Marty" Enos	Stokerman	29	Cheboygan, Mich.
Erhardt Felax†	Stokerman	46	Rogers City, Mich.
Cleland Gager†	Oiler	30	Onaway, Mich.
Paul Greengtski	Watchman	23	Rogers City, Mich.
Paul Heller†	Stokerman	45	Rogers City, Mich.
Paul Horn†	Oiler	21	Rogers City, Mich.

Dennis Joppich	Wiper	19	Rogers City, Mich.
Raymond Kowalski†	Wheelsman	31	Rogers City, Mich.
Joseph Krawczak†	Wheelsman	35	Rogers City, Mich.
Floyd MacDougall	Oiler	26	Rogers City, Mich.
Frank Mays	Deckwatchman	26	Rogers City, Mich.
Dennis Meredith	Deckhand	25	Metz, Mich.
Melville Orr	Watchman	35	Rogers City, Mich.
Alfred Pilarski†	Second Cook	30	Rogers City, Mich.
Gary Price†	Deckhand	21	Onaway, Mich.
Leo Promo, Jr.†	Asst. Conveyorman	21	Rogers City, Mich.
Bernard Schefke†	Porter	19	Rogers City, Mich.
James Selke	Porter	18	Rogers City, Mich.
Gary Strzelecki†	Deckwatchman	21	Rogers City, Mich.
Earl Tulgetske, Jr.	Wheelsman	30	Rogers City, Mich.
Edward Vallee†	Conveyorman	49	Rogers City, Mich.
John Zoho†	Steward	63	Claireton, Penn.

* Survivors (2); † Recovered bodies (18); Missing (15)

BIBLIOGRAPHY

BOOKS

Clary, James. *Ladies of the Lakes.* Lansing, Mich.: Woolly Bear Productions, 1981.

Hancock, Paul. *Shipwrecks of the Great Lakes.* San Diego: Thunder Bay Press, 2001.

Hatcher, Harlan, and Erich A. Walter. *A Pictorial History of the Great Lakes.* New York: Crown Publishing, 1963.

Havighurst, Walter. *The Long Ships Passing: The Story of the Great Lakes.* New York: Macmillan, 1975.

Hemming, Robert J. *Gales of November: The Sinking of the* Edmund Fitzgerald. Chicago: Contemporary Books, 1981.

Mays, Frank, Jim Stayer, Pat Stayer, and Tim Juhl. *If We Make it 'til Daylight: The Story of Frank Mays.* Lexington, Mich.: Out of the Blue Productions, 2003.

Micketti, Gerald F. *The Bradley Boats.* Traverse City, Mich.: G. F. Micketti, 1995.

Ratigan, William. *Great Lakes Shipwrecks and Survivals.* New York: Galahad Books, 1994.

Rogers City: Its First 100 Years. Rogers City, Mich.: Presque Isle County Historical Society, 1971.

Thompson, Mark L. *Graveyard of the Lakes.* Detroit: Wayne State University Press, 2000.

NEWSPAPER ARTICLES

"Can History Repeat?" *Alpena News*, November 19, 1988, 6B.

"Coast Guard Starts Probe of Sinking." *Traverse City Record-Eagle*, November 20, 1958, 1.

"Dead Are Laid to Rest as Community Mourns." *Presque Isle County Advance,* November 27, 1958.

"Early Storm Lashes West, Rolls Across the Midwest." *Traverse City Record-Eagle*, November 18, 1958, 1.

"A Few Minutes Changed Lives." *Alpena News*, November 19, 1988, 6B.

"Freighter with 35 Feared Lost in Gale on Lake Michigan." *New York Times*, November 19, 1958, 1.

"German Skipper Describes Sinking of *Carl Bradley.*" *Traverse City Record-Eagle*, November 21, 1958, 7.

"Here is What Happened." *Presque Isle County Advance,* November 27, 1958, 2.

"Heroic Doctor, 79, Was Ready to Risk Life to Save Crewman." *Traverse City Record-Eagle*, November 20, 1958, 7.

"Hope Dims for 15 Missing Seamen: Two Survivors Tell of Ordeal." *Traverse City Record-Eagle*, November 20, 1958, 1.

"Hope is Given Up for 15 Missing in Shipwreck." *Los Angeles Times*, November 21, 1958, 16.

"Mayday!" *Alpena News*, November 19, 1988, 6B.

"Michigan Mourns Her Sailor Sons." *Detroit Free Press*, November 19, 1958. Rpt. *Presque Isle County Advance,* November 27, 1958.

"'No Lifeboats Visible': 35 Missing as Ship Splits in Two, Sinks." *Los Angeles Times,* November 19, 1958, 1.

"Only Two Survive Lake Shipwreck." *New York Times,* November 20, 1958, 39.

"Rogers City—A Town Numbed with Grief." *Traverse City Record-Eagle*, November 20, 1958, 1.

"Ship Sinks in Storm; No Trace of 37 Found." *The Washington Post and Times Herald*, November 19, 1958, A1.

"Ship Victims Buried Today." *Traverse City Record-Eagle*, November 22, 1958.

"*Str. Bradley* Sinks with 35 Aboard: Death Strikes Many of These Homes." *Presque Isle County Advance,* November 20, 1958, 1.

"Two Men Saved, Nine Bodies Sighted in Lake Michigan Freighter Disaster." *Traverse City Record-Eagle*, November 19, 1958, 1.

"2 Survivors of Sinking Reach Port in Michigan." *The Washington Post and Times Herald*, November 20, 1958, A1, A7.

ENCYCLOPEDIAS, MAGAZINES, AND PERIODICALS

Ashlee, Laura R. "Broken in Two: The Wreck of the *Carl D. Bradley*." *Michigan History* 74, no. 6 (1990): 32–37.

"Children's Fund Established." *ML Screenings* (Winter 1958–59):, 14.

"Coast Guard Spearheads Rescue Effort." *ML Screenings* (Winter 1958–59): 6–7.

"Great Lakes." *Compton's Encyclopedia*, vol. 9 (Chicago: Compton's Learning Company, 1994).

Kloster, J. "The Wreck of the *Carl D. Bradley*." *Anchor News* 18, no. 5 (1987): 72–76.

"Lake Michigan." *Microsoft Encarta Encyclopedia Standard Edition 2004* (Redmond, Wash.: Microsoft, 1993–2003).

Renwick, William H. "Great Lakes." *Microsoft Encarta Encyclopedia Standard Edition 2004.* (Redmond, Wash.: Microsoft Corporation, 1993–2003).

"Steamer *Carl D. Bradley* Lost in Lake Michigan Storm." *ML Screenings* (Winter 1958–59): 3–5.

Stein, Janis. "Shipwreck Survivor Tells His Story." *The Lakeshore Guardian* 6, no. 1 (January 2004) at www.lakeshoreguardian.com.

"Storm and Death on a Great Lake." *Life* 45 (December 1, 1958): 26–33.

U.S. GOVERNMENT INVESTIGATIVE REPORTS

Marine Casualty Report: S.S. Carl D. Bradley. Washington, D.C.: U.S. Coast Guard, July 7, 1959.

Ship's Log: U.S. Coast Guard Cutter Sundew (WAGL 404), November 1958.

INTERVIEWS

Enos, Janet L. Telephone interview with the author. 2 March 2006.

Horn, Charlie and Nancy. Personal interview with author. Rogers City, Michigan. 24 June 2004 and 22 January 2005.

Kowalski, Betty and Bob. Personal interview with author. Rogers City, Michigan. 22 January 2005.

Maldonado, Laural (curator, Presque Isle County Historical Museum). Personal interview with author. Rogers City, Michigan. 24 June 2004.

McCown, Sam. Telephone interview with author. 28 January 2005.

INTERNET, DVD, AND VIDEO SOURCES

"*Carl D. Bradley.*" Marine Historical Society of Detroit.

Carl D. Bradley*: 40th Anniversary Remembrance.* VHS. Lexington, Mich.: Out of the Blue Productions, 1999.

Deep Adventure: A Dive to the Carl D. Bradley. DVD. Lexington, Mich.: Out of the Blue Productions, 2003.

"Frank Mays Visits Shipwreck Museum: Survivor of the *Carl D. Bradley.*" *Shipwreck Stories Archives.* May 1, 2001.

"Lake Michigan Facts and Figures." *Great Lakes Information Network.* 1993–2004.

Remembering the Carl D. Bradley. DVD. Hosted by Doug Petcash and produced and directed by photojournalist Corey Adkins, WWTV/WWUP-TV 9 and 10 News. Cadillac, Mich.: Heritage Broadcasting Company of Michigan, 2004.

"Shorelines of the Great Lakes." Department of Environmental Quality, State of Michigan. 2001–2004.

"Survivor Recalls Sinking of the *Novadoc*–November 11, 1940." Lloyd Belcher's account. *Shipwreck Stories Archives.* February 22, 2001.

The Wreck of the Carl D. Bradley. VHS. Kenosha, Wisc.: Southport Video Productions, 2001.